Elliott Carter

A Centennial Celebration

Elliott Carter

Elliott Carter

A Centennial Celebration

edited by

Marc Ponthus
and Susan Tang

FESTSCHRIFT SERIES No. 23

PENDRAGON PRESS
HILLSDALE, NEW YORK

Other Titles in the Festschrift Series

No. 1	Musical Offering Essays in Honor of Martin Bernstein
No. 2	Aspects of Medieval and Renaissance Music A Birthday Offering To Gustave Reese
No. 3	Music East & West Essays in Honor of Walter Kaufmann
No. 4	Essays On The Music of J. S. Bach and Other Divers Subjects A Tribute To Gerhard Herz
No. 5	Music in The Classic Period: Essays in Honor of Barry S. Brook
No. 6	Five Centuries of Choral Music: Essays in Honor of Howard Swan
No. 7	Explorations in Music, the Arts, and Ideas: Essays in Honor of Leonard B. Meyer
No. 8	Modern Music Librarianship: Essays in Honor of Ruth Watanabe
No. 9	Libraries, History, Diplomacy, and the Performing Arts: Essays in Honor of Carleton Sprague Smith
No. 10	Convention In 18th- And 19th-Century Music: Essays in Honor of Leonard G. Ratner
No. 11	Musical Humanism and Its Legacy: Essays in Honor of Claude Palisca
No. 12	The Organist as Scholar: Essays in Memory of Russell Saunders
No. 13	Eighteenth-century Music in Theory and Practice: Essays in Honor of Alfred Mann
No. 14	Festa Musicologica: Essays in Honor of George Buelow
No. 15	Pianist, Scholar, Connoisseur: Essays in Honor of Jacob Lateiner
No. 16	Liber Amicorum John Steele: A Musicological Tribute
No. 17	Encomium Musicae: A Festschrift in Honor of Robert J. Snow
No. 18	Musica Franca: Essays in Honor of Frank A. D'Accone
No. 19	Liber amicorum Isabelle Cazeaux: Symbols, Parallels and Discoveries in Her Honor
No. 20	Words on Music: Essays in honor of Andrew Porter
No. 21	Remembering Oliver Strunk: Teacher and Scholar

Cover design by Stuart Ross

Cover photo courtesy of Nicole Rzewski

Library of Congress Cataloging-in-Publication Data

Elliott Carter : a centennial celebration / edited by Marc Ponthus and Susan Tang.

p. cm. -- (Festschrift series ; no. 23)

ISBN 978-1-57647-135-7 (alk. paper)

1. Carter, Elliott, 1908---Criticism and interpretation. 2. Music--20th century--History and criticism. I. Carter, Elliott, 1908- II. Ponthus, Marc. III. Tang, Susan, 1980-

ML410.C3293E66 2008

780.92--dc22

2008027042

Copyright Pendragon Press 2008

Contents

Illustrations	vi
Preface	ix
Conversation with Pierre Boulez	1
On Carter's Influence by Fred Lerdahl	15
"Its full choir of echoes" The composer in his library by Paul Griffiths	23
E Poi by Alvin Curran	41
✷ On Elliott Carter's "Anaphora" from *A Mirror on Which to Dwell* by Louis Karchin	47
Elliott Carter: The Sustained Line by Charles Rosen	59
Souvenirs by Frederic Rzewski	65
Beginnings and Endings – Plus a Conversation by Richard Wilson	75
Elliott Carter (A Centennial Tribute) by John Ashbery followed by *Syringa*	99
Metric Modulation by Walter Zimmerman	107
Chronological List of Elliott Carter Works	121

Illustrations

Elliott Carter	ii
Elliott Carter	vi
Sir William Glock, Pierre Boulez, and Elliott Carter at the awarding of the Ernst Von Sieman's Prize, Munich, 1981	14
Beethoven's Fifth Symphony, I, bars 6-21	16
Carter's Second Quartet, bars 57-61	17
Fred Lerdahl's Oboe Quartet, pages 1 and 2	21, 22
Am Klavier	34-40
e poi by Alvin Curran	44, 45
Examples from Carter's *Anphora*	48-50
Louis Karchen's *Songs of Keats*, pp. 1 and 2	55, 56
Charles Rosen and Elliott Carter	58
Examples from Carter's Piano Sonata	59-63
Elliott Carter and Frederic Rzewski, Berlin 1963	66
Elliott Carter with Ursala Oppens and Frederic Rzewski	71
Frederic Rzewski's *"96,"* pp. 1 and 2	72, 73
Clarinet Concerto by Elliott Carter, meas. 444-447	83
Asko Concerto by Elliott Carter meas. 290-296	84, 85
Boston Concerto by Elliott Carter meas. 354-358	86
Symphony of Three Orchestras by Elliott Carter meas. 1-5	87
Asko Concerto by Elliott Carter meas. 1-6	88
Boston Concerto by Elliott Carter meas. 1-4	89
Boston Concerto by Elliott Carter meas. 14-19	90
Dialogues for Piano and Orchestra by Elliott Carter meas. 12-18	91
Dialogues for Piano and Orchestra by Elliott Carter meas. 19-24	92
What Next? by Elliott Carter meas. 35-	93
What Next? by Elliott Carter meas. 994-998	94
Richard Wilson's *Gravitas*	95, 96
Metric Modulation	108-111
Elliott Carter's String Quartet No. 1	112-117
Walter Zimmerman's *As I was Walking I came upon Chance*	118, 119

Preface

by Marc Ponthus

"for the self must penetrate and digest all the richness of its substance" – G.W.F. Hegel

"when the very white cliffs emerged from the shimmering in the furthest backgrounds of the sea, Vezzano appeared curiously near" – Julien Gracq.

The significance of Elliott Carter's longevity is more fundamental than the mere numbering of his years. Any work that has to do with performance enters a space-perception of real time. Music, simply through the minutia of its language, intensifies real time. In Carter's music, to speak simply of real time would be not only reductive, but also deceptive. His work engages perception of time on planes of complexity, and alters that perception. It interacts, unravels, finds its existential episteme in time and with time. The way in which the language of Carter and the specificity of its syntax and process, developed through many years, brings another stratum of experience of time.

The cultural territory from which Carter's work arises is particularly vast, through an insatiable curiosity as much as a considerable knowledge, but also through the openness of his mind. He acknowledges particular interests in disparate and apparently complementary areas of musical creation, and in composers of the past as much as in his contemporaries, and the younger generation. However, when looking at his work, it is impossible to find specific musical influences, even if one is generally aware that much material has been absorbed. The temptation is to look outside music to identify, or imagine, affinities and resonances of vision. As I am writing these words, a score of the *Triple Duo* sits on top of a pile of papers. On the evening of the presentation in New York of this book to Elliott Carter (at the Great Hall at Cooper Union), I will be conducting this work. Written for a small ensemble, it explores fundamental aspects of the complexity of his language, what is often referred to as simultaneous streams, interacting with metric modulations. The relationship of process, formal process and its constructive elements and details, is striking in the degree of precision of its notation. Thinking outside music, looking at the language from a perspective that could be semiotic as much as architectural, one could almost see an exquisite geometrization of that language, the working with the planes of time evoking affinities with Deleuze's *becomings*, appearing to evolve a sort of articulated geomorphology. There is a tangible awareness of an exceptionally lucid mind at work.

Elliott Carter

© 2000 Meredith Heuer, courtesy Boosey & Hawkes, Inc.

A Conversation with Pierre Boulez

Marc Ponthus

Today is April 12, 2007. We are here in Berlin at the *Staatsoper* to talk about the work and life of Elliott Carter who will turn 100 years old in 2008. M. Boulez, do you have any reflections about what it is like for an artist to be working at this age? I can only think of the 16th century painter, Titian, and presently, the film director Manuel de Olivera, who worked into their mid-nineties. Does his age and experience of so many life events throughout the years, bring a particular understanding of the world? What are your thoughts?

Pierre Boulez

I think he represents a resume of the century. He successfully went through many periods in the history of music…but, as you know, in some ways, he was a late beginner. Comparing his compositional development, for example, with (Olivier Messiaen's) development, Messiaen developed and discovered a full compositional vocabulary when he was still quite young, but after approximately the age of fifty, even though not repeating himself, he did not change his style, he maintained the same high level of writing, using his creativity to combine the same type of elements until the end of his life. On the contrary, in my opinion, Elliott Carter began with some uncertainty. He was first attracted by the American avant-garde of the Twenties. He then went to Paris like many American musicians to study with Nadia Boulanger, where he was influenced by the Stravinskian Neoclassicism. His writing had always been meticulous; but in the late 40's and early 50's he discovered his real compositional voice and became much more adventurous. In the last 50 years, he has worked very hard, at first at a slow pace on works of extreme complexity. Then, he became more flexible, very inventive, less complicated, easier to perform as a consequence. He has since then never stopped. I am amazed…everybody is amazed that he still composes and creates so many new works.

Marc Ponthus

You had made a comment some years ago that even though he is almost 20 years older than you, he is more of your generation than of his own.

Pierre Boulez

That's true and I find his works very interesting. It is not just production, but in each work he tries to solve not a problem…when you use the word "problem" you immediately think of a mathematical equation…rather he gives solutions to things. He's always thinking and remains very inventive. For me, his works are always a source of reflection, I not only like to read but also to conduct his works because I very often learn something.

Marc Ponthus

Could you expand on that?

Pierre Boulez

I find his rhythmic modulation something that really belongs to him, although Igor Stravinsky used it. In Stravinsky's ballet *Les Noces*, you always have these modulations, on a very simple basis, 3 to 2, or 3 to 4, but with Elliott Carter, although it is the same principle, it is much more complex. He made me discover the composer Conlon Nancarrow, who was not well known at all, other than in very small circles. He was not so much influenced but rather excited by Nancarrow, who composed, as you know, for the mechanical piano. Nowadays, you have people adapting his music for other instruments, which is rather utopian; the fact that he composed for mechanical piano implies that it is specifically for this medium and not for all sort of instruments. Although he was aware of people like Charles Ives he was not influenced at all by the idea of collage or the use of popular songs. What interested him in Charles Ives was the vocabulary, a kind of research that is improvised each time; there was imagination there. This is what influenced him.

Marc Ponthus

I find it striking that in the late 40's and early 50's when Elliott Carter's vocabulary was not yet fully developed, you and Karlheinz Stockhausen were writing major works. Although he was older and at that time not quite in the *avant-garde*, he did ultimately move into it, the same way a young composer would, may we say, fearlessly?

Pierre Boulez

I remember in 1955 at an ISCM (International Society for Contemporary Music) festival in Baden Baden, Germany, the year my own Marteau sans Maître was first performed. In another of those concerts, the Sonata for Cello and Piano by Elliott Carter was also performed. It was an "in-between" work because it was in the neo-classical style, but there was also something else in it that was really striking. Later, I was organizing the concerts of Domaine Musical in Paris where the Parenin Quartet (the first violin's name was Parenin) told me "Oh, we have discovered a string quartet by somebody called Elliott Carter. Could you put that on the program if it is of interest to you?" I saw the score and said yes, I think it was the first time Elliott Carter was performed in that circle. I was later introduced to the Double Concerto by our mutual friend William Glock, the controller of the BBC.

Marc Ponthus

But this is very much later, isn't it?

Pierre Boulez

Yes, I think it was around 1965. There were many steps between the *Sonata for Cello and Piano* and the *Double Concerto*. A lot of water under the bridge, as one says. I was amazed that although he was not our companion, he had his own language that was very different than what we were doing, we being Karlheinz Stockhausen, Luciano Berio, myself and so on. His music was highly complex, the organization was very interesting and from that moment I became keenly interested in Elliott Carter. Later on, I also began to know him more closely than when I was in New York. Back in Paris, the Ensemble Intercontemporain regularly commissioned pieces of his. We always perform his work and continue to do so regularly because he is one of the most important composers for the ensemble.

Marc Ponthus

Allow me to move back a little. When was the first time you heard a piece of Elliott Carter?

Pierre Boulez

It was the *Sonata for Cello and Piano*.

Marc Ponthus

Did you meet him at the time?

Pierre Boulez

Well, I met him. He remembers but I don't remember myself very precisely. He told me about the encounter in Baden-Baden. I do remember meeting him later when I was in New York

Marc Ponthus

He told me about hearing *Marteau sans Maître*, although I do not remember if it was on that particular occasion in Baden-Baden. I wonder with influences going back and forth between composers, do you see any influence of *Marteau* in the works of Carter?

Pierre Boulez

Yes, only it was much later in the piece, *A Mirror in which to Dwell*, it is a mixture between *Pierrot Lunaire* and *Marteau sans Maître*. I think there is one other piece for viola, xylophone and flute that's very close in sound to *Marteau*, but not anything else.

Marc Ponthus

Would it have something to do with the relationship of register?

Pierre Boulez

Maybe, but I think he is terribly independent. I don't think many things influenced him, he concentrated on himself and his vocabulary. It is not really the style but rather the approach of the harmonic language that is similar between us. For instance, there is a book published on harmony by Elliott Carter where accumulations of chords are derived from each other. I have used the same method to make the register function at the same time, that's certainly something similar. He organizes that before writing, then he writes with this kind of grid. I myself sometimes use this type of grid to orient the ear to the register I want to use. It is not a stylistic influence we share but rather a kind of process.

Marc Ponthus

About analysis—he is not too keen about analyzing his work.

Pierre Boulez

Nor am I. I made some analysis of rather simple pieces but if you have to explain everything then…you don't need that, if somebody else wants to do it, that's fine. Even if the analysis is wrong, I prefer an interesting wrong analysis, than a right analysis that is not interesting.

Marc Ponthus

A different perspective, of course.

Pierre Boulez

If you open a new perspective that is more interesting than just being literally exact.

Marc Ponthus

There was a conversation between Elliott Carter and Charles Rosen where Elliott was interested by a theory of recurrence of pitch that Charles Rosen went into. Moving back, did you conduct the *Double Concerto*?

Pierre Boulez

Yes.

Marc Ponthus

Who were the soloists?

Pierre Boulez

Paul Jacobs plus Charles Rosen….no, it was not Charles Rosen but Ursula Oppens…Paul Jacobs and Ursula Oppens.

Marc Ponthus

A personal curiosity, as a conductor, do you independently conduct the two ensembles in that piece?

Pierre Boulez

At the end, yes.

Marc Ponthus

What about the 3 against 4?

Pierre Boulez

You have to learn some pages of score from memory. When you don't have a third hand or another musician turning the pages, and have to conduct with both hands, you have to memorize…it's not very long, maybe two or three pages of score.

Marc Ponthus

You said that you do not remember well the first meeting. When did you meet personally in a more meaningful kind of manner?

Pierre Boulez

It came progressively. I was already very familiar with him when I invited him to Cleveland. I did some evenings, explaining the work of a composer, and I did two of them in the same year in Cleveland, that was in '70 or '71. I did one on Edgar Varèse and one on Elliott Carter and I invited him to explain, to give some examples. It was the Concerto for Orchestra I guess, and then I asked him to present it to the audience. We explained the complex piece and I also explained the difficulties of performing and after that we performed the piece entirely. It was very interesting at this period and I knew him then very well.

Marc Ponthus

Is Carter the American composer you have performed most?

Pierre Boulez

Definitely. He's the American composer who certainly interests me the most…by far.

Marc Ponthus

I know that even though he is American, he carries a strong European affinity.

Pierre Boulez

Yes, that is not untrue. Among the American composers, he's certainly the most European cultivated. He has more European culture than American. His only truly American moment was Pocahontas, at this period (c.1939), all American composers tried to be genuinely "American". I organized a mini festival focused on the works of Charles Ives when I was with the New York Philharmonic. It was a study of the evolution of the arts, not only in music but also painting during the 20's and 30's, especially during the Great Depression. During this time, this evolution was parallel to what happened in the Soviet Union, there was a need to be populist, culture had to be accessible to everyone. There was also a change in Russia and there was very strong political pressure in the Soviet Union but in America that was under a kind of New Deal depression expression! An example is Aaron Copland, who wrote Piano Variations and the

Short Symphony, which were very much under the influence of Stravinsky, and then suddenly wrote music that was folk music that was suppose to make people dance and be very cheerful. This period corresponded to the paintings at Rockefeller Center that were similar to the populist paintings found in Mexico during the same period. That was the only period when Elliott Carter had a moment of populist culture in his output. After the war, it was very different. It was interesting to read the articles he wrote for a new music magazine. I don't remember the title, but it was a magazine about new music and he regularly wrote reviews of concerts of contemporary music, you could really see his taste changing progressively.

Marc Ponthus

Perspectives of New Music?

Pierre Boulez

No, *Perspectives of New Music* was later, that was the team of Milton Babbitt. No, it was a magazine at the end of the '30's. [1]

Marc Ponthus

What do you feel your many performances of his music have accomplished, for the public? Do you have a sense of that on the American or the European audiences?

Pierre Boulez

All of Elliott Carter's works pointed towards looking for his own vocabulary. They are a kind of process of research, always looking for something, and they are sometimes rather difficult to understand. The way of looking at the structure of the music is stronger than the feeling itself. Sometimes the vocabulary is very complex, you may not understand it fully immediately, you have to listen to it a couple of times. I remember it was difficult to perform his music. If you only have the usual number of rehearsals that American orchestras typically do, it is very difficult to put on a very good performance. Because of the difficulty, I prefer to conduct his chamber works for an ensemble of 25-30. With that size, you have the opportunity to rehearse in small groups and truly solve the difficulties, with everybody there. There is flexibility with the rehearsal time. This is why I play his works regularly with the Ensemble Intercontemporain, the more you perform the works, the more it becomes easy for the performers

[1] *Modern Music, 1924-1946*

to bring the music to the audience. For instance, when we did the *Clarinet Concerto* for four or five groups, the first performance was a real performance, not at all an experience where you are trying to find your way in a thick forest.

Marc Ponthus

Do you have plans to revisit some of his works you have conducted?

Pierre Boulez

Oh yes, we will do a concert for his 100th birthday. There is a commission that he is writing for Daniel Barenboim at the piano, and I will conduct the orchestra.

Marc Ponthus

You have written works for him and he has written works for you. Could you speak about that a little?

Pierre Boulez

Yes, we are good friends and the 17 or 20 year difference doesn't matter. There is always a homage for round figures, as one says, I wrote something for his 80th and 90th birthdays. Then he also wrote for my birthday, generally as an exchange of gifts. I sometimes used the birthday to make a much longer work. For *Dérive II*, which was written for his 80th birthday, it was actually finished for his 95th birthday. I was confident in his health, and knew it could stand for so many years.

Marc Ponthus

There is also the interest in literature that you both share. He was in Paris when the work of Marcel Proust was being first published and he is also very interested in James Joyce as you are. Do you have a different approach from him?

Pierre Boulez

I think in *Ulysses*, James Joyce looks at the technique of each chapter where each chapter has a kind of story. I think James Joyce is the equivalent of Wozzeck. For instance, you have the chapter with questions, answers, you have the references to the evolution of the language and so on and so forth. In each chapter of Wozzeck you have also the same, you have 5 pre-classical forms, 5 symphonic forms, and 5 inventions. This technique gives each scene of Wozzeck a specific character and in James Joyce, it is exactly the same. In Marcel Proust it is much more complex, in a way, because the style is not so clearly visible. You have the evolution of a character where, as you approach the ending, you become more interested in the retrospect of the story. There are also all kinds of diversions such as reflections on paintings, references to the novel itself, how the novel was written, literature, and so on and so forth. At the beginning, Marcel Proust is telling you a story and the more he goes, the more he reflects on the story he is thinking of writing, because it is always in the future. And then he writes about the things he is encountering which help him to further the story. In Elliott Carter you have more influence of Marcel Proust than James Joyce. He is telling his musical stories, where, in a way, you are closer to the discovery of retrospect as you are going forward.

Marc Ponthus

As far as James Joyce, you don't find any influence of the language itself on Elliott Carter? Even aurally, a certain fluidity of language?

Pierre Boulez

No, maybe it's just me, but I don't find any resemblances between the language of James Joyce and the language of Elliott Carter. The language in literature is so different from the language of music.

Marc Ponthus

The complexity of rhythm is of course one of the most striking aspects of Elliott Carter's music. This complexity can be seen as a way to write rhythmically different tempi or to write a certain flow of tempi through rhythm, which would be different. Do you see it that way?

Pierre Boulez

Yes, there is certainly differences of speed, I would like to say, simply the speed you can really hear when you have regular units because then you can really recognize the speed if you have varying positions of speed. I find the early works of Elliott Carter that use this technique easier to listen to than the later works, where he uses rhythmic patterns with holes. An example of this is in a quintuplet, where you have two notes and the fifth note with nothing in between. The problem is recognizing the quintuplet, if you are too refined in a definite speed, the refinement can apply to any speed. When I wrote my piece *Rituel*, I used a regular unit for each group where this regular unit is constantly interrupted and pushed forwards and backwards. You can hear the difference in the pulse because you hear the regular pulse in different moments. It is similar in *Gruppen* by Stockhausen where it is difficult to identify the type of speed because the writing is refined in each layer. It's interesting, but more chaotic as an impression, rather than as a super imposition of speeds.

Marc Ponthus

Is it connected with timbre also? I'm thinking of the *Triple Duo* where the three different rhythmic patterns are very clear.

Pierre Boulez

Yes, but that's much later in his work because he certainly was more aware of the difficulty of superimposing the various speeds.

Marc Ponthus

Did the language become clearer later on?

Pierre Boulez

The language became clearer, his late works are much easier to perform than the earlier works.

Marc Ponthus

Do you have a similar development in your music?

Pierre Boulez

Yes, especially as a conductor, I am aware of the difficulty of what you perceive and what you don't perceive. If you want something not to be perceived then you can do it. I am not against the fact that you always have to be clear. But if you want to be clear, you have to be aware of the difficulties.

Marc Ponthus

Clarity is very important for you, I believe.

Pierre Boulez

Yes, of course.

Marc Ponthus

Perhaps in Elliott Carter it is not as primary?

Pierre Boulez

I think he wants to be understood. Who does not want to be understood?

Marc Ponthus

Yes, but I am thinking of the clarity of….

Pierre Boulez

Texture?

Marc Ponthus

Perhaps, it is more in the clarity of gesture than the texture. Sometimes the complexity of the texture and polyphony is not so clear, but the texture has an energy of its own.

Pierre Boulez

You have moments, for instance, in the most difficult works, like his *Concerto for Orchestra*, where there is a big brass solo — that is very obvious because the writing simplified. Then you have other moments when it is difficult because of the superimposition of very different layers and you have to find your way in the middle of it.

Marc Ponthus

To finish, I remember Elliott Carter saying that he was impressed after hearing *Marteau sans Maître* and although he didn't grasp it immediately, he later got into it. If we reverse that, I'm wondering, since he wrote an opera at 90 years old, does that give you some ideas for your future works?

Pierre Boulez

Well, maybe. There are two people with whom I tried to work with. First Jean Genet and he died, second was Heiner Müller, and he died too…so I did not try a third for the time being. I have thought of music for the theater but I don't think I would be very happy with the normal way of putting music in a theater with a pit, a stage and so on. I would like an open hall that can distribute the music as you want and to be able to think of music in space immediately. They have done quite a lot in spoken theater to expand the idea of theater. Of course, you do not have the acoustical problems of music, and you can have people in every corner. They are freer than we are as musician. If I do something for theatre, if I ever do, it will be with a reflection on how to conceive the theater, because I find myself very interested and much in love with the theater of Asia, with Bunraku, Kabuki and so on. There are things we have never done in our Western tradition because of the acoustical conditions. Now, with microphones, amplification, and modification of sound, you can put the sound wherever you want. The orchestra pit is not satisfying to me. When I did *Répons*, which does not accommodate a hall, you have to either transform the hall or to have an empty space. I would like to do for the theatre what did for *Répons*.

Marc Ponthus

In the greater sense, since Elliott Carter did something entirely new for him at 90 years old, are you ready to do something completely new as well?

Pierre Boulez

I suppose so, but I will tell you in 10 years!

* * * * *

Biography

Since conducting his first concerts when barely out of his 20s, Pierre Boulez has become one of the foremost composer/conductors since Richard Strauss and one of the most influential musical figures of this century.

Born in 1925, he studied piano as a boy before moving to Paris in 1942 where he continued his studies at the Paris Conservatory with Messiaen, Andrée Vaurabourg, and René Leibowitz. In 1946 he became Music Director of the Renaud-Barrault Theatre Company and in 1953 founded the contemporary music series at the Petit Marigny Theatre, which developed into the renowned and influential Domaine Musical.

During the late 1950s, he gave courses at the progressive Darmstadt summer school and then at Basle University, whilst at the same time continuing his work both as composer and conductor. In the academic year 1962-63 he was Visiting Professor at Harvard University and in 1976 was appointed Professor at the Collège de France, a post he held until retirement in 1995.

In 1967 Pierre Boulez became Principal Guest Conductor of the Cleveland Orchestra later accepting the positions of Chief Conductor of the BBC Symphony Orchestra and Music Director of the New York Philharmonic. One year later, in 1972, he accepted the invitation of the French President to create and direct the Institut de Recherche et de Coordination Acoustique/Musique (IRCAM), the computer-music research centre in Paris, followed by founding the *Ensemble intercontemporain*.

Widely regarded as one of the leading interpreters of the music of the Second Viennese School - Schoenberg, Berg and Webern - Pierre Boulez is also renowned for his many performances and recordings of the music of Wagner, Mahler, Stravinsky, Bartók, Debussy, Ravel and Messiaen. He has conducted Parsifal and the Ring in Bayreuth, an award-winning *Pelléas et Mélisande* for Welsh National Opera and *Duke Bluebeard's Castle* at the Aix-en-Provence Festival.

In 1995 he undertook a major tour with the London Symphony Orchestra to celebrate his 70th birthday, as well as in 2000 and 2005 to celebrate his 75th and 80th birthdays. Recent engagements have included concerts in Paris, Chicago, New York, Cleveland, Vienna, Lucerne and London.

Sir William Glock, Pierre Boulez, and Elliott Carter at the awarding of the
Ernst Von Sieman's Prize, Munich, 1981

Photo by Anne Kirchbach

On Carter's Influence

Fred Lerdahl

The music of Elliott Carter has been a continuous presence in my life since I was a teenager. My point of entry was the Second String Quartet, which will be my primary reference in these remarks. I listened to this work countless times in the early 1960s, from the first recording by the Juilliard Quartet. I was fascinated by the music's sonorities and flow, and I tried to make sense of its difficulties. Since then I have periodically returned to Carter's music. As much as any contemporary American composer, he has continued and renewed the tradition of non-programmatic modernist music. I see my own work as belonging in many respects to that tradition, and I admire the grandeur with which he has carried out his project.

Carter's music has influenced me in four fundamental ways. The first has affected many composers: his treatment of musical time, in particular the interplay of multiple tempi as a structural and expressive device. Essential to his method is metric modulation, in which one or more instrument sets a new tempo, as a sort of pivot, as the previous tempo concludes. This technique might more accurately be referred to as tempo modulation, since the musical entities in question are competing pulsations rather than competing metrical grids (the latter as in the famous ballroom scene in *Don Giovanni*). It could be said that Carter replaces vertical metrical complexity with horizontal tempo complexity. That is, in Mozart or Beethoven we hear many metrical levels at once and in the same overall tempo, whereas in Carter we hear simultaneous pulsations (single metrical levels, if you like) going at multiple speeds.

As illustration, Figure 1 gives the metrical grid for bars 6-21 of the first movement of Beethoven's Fifth Symphony. The musical surface is mostly made up of eighth and half notes, but as listeners we infer in-phase periodicities not only at these durational levels but also at the half-bar, 2-bar, 4-bar, and even 8-bar levels. The larger metrical levels are inferred not by durational patterns but by harmonic rhythm and parallelism. In the grid notation, each periodicity is represented by a row of dots, with the time spans between dots indicated by the note values at the left. A beat that is strong at one level is also a beat at the next larger level. In Figure 1, the second and fourth eighths of each bar receive one dot, the first and third eighths two dots, the downbeat of each bar three dots, the downbeats

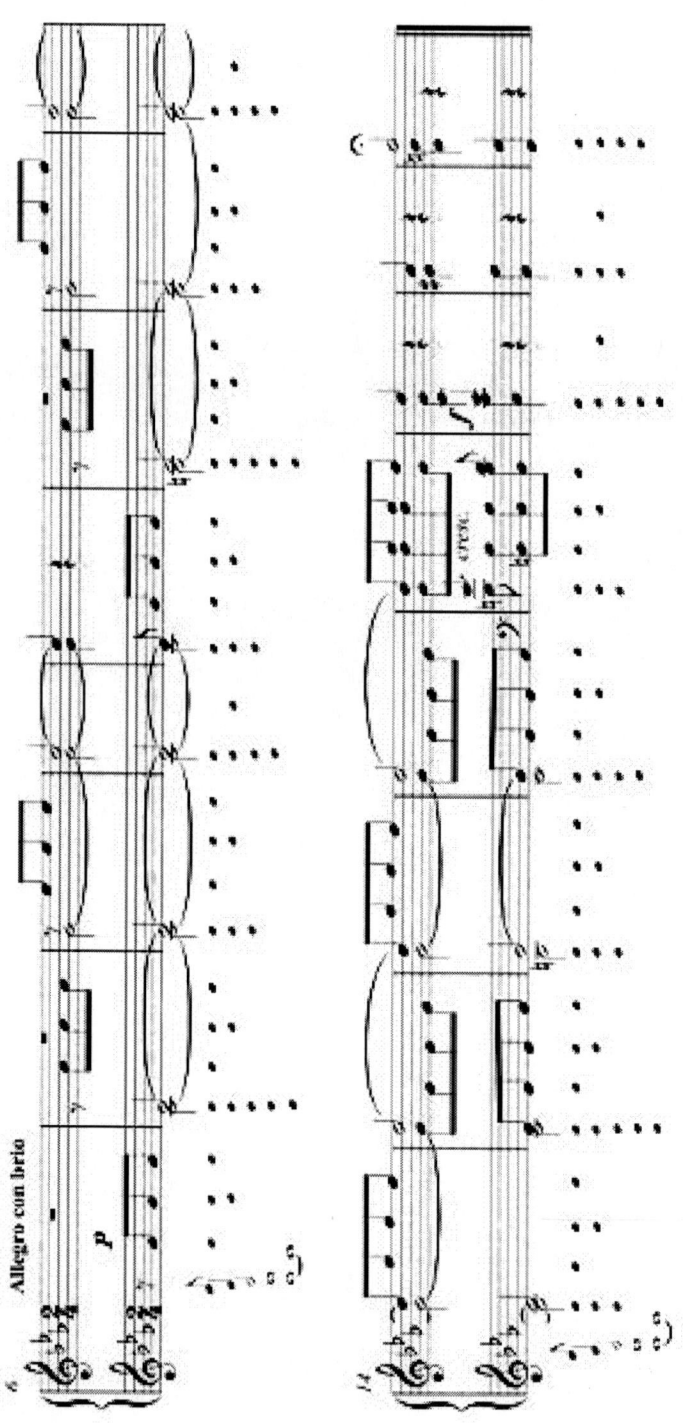

Figure 1: Beethoven's Fifth Symphony, I, bars 6-21

Figure 2: Carter's Second Quartet, bars 57-61

Copyright © 1961 (Renewed) by Associated Music Publishers, Inc. (BMI) International Copyright Secured. All Rights Reserved. Used by Permission.

of odd-numbered bars four dots, and the downbeats of bars 7, 11, 15, and 19 five dots. This is a case of vertical metrical depth.

In contrast to Figure 1, the rhythmic patterns in Figure 2, bars 57-61 of Carter's Second Quartet, do not line up and reinforce one another. Rather, each instrument moves at its own tempo. Specifically, the quintuplet sixteenths in the first violin correspond to metronome marking 560 (five times the notated tempo of mm. 112); the staccato chords in the second violin are at mm. 70 (consistently so through the tempo modulations); the triplet eighths in the viola are at mm. 336; and the cello accelerates from mm. 74.7 to mm. 186.7. This is a case of horizontal tempo complexity. The notational complication arises from the necessity to relate the four tempi to one another. A given tempo is chosen as the frame within which the other tempi relate, and the frame changes through tempo modulation. Although there is only one referential tempo at any given moment, the real point is the coexistence of the multiple tempi themselves.

Carter lays out his tempo relationships with rhetorical and expressive purpose. The varying degree of complexity of the tempo relationships helps project his ideas in waves of increasing and decreasing tension: the more complex the tempo relationships, the denser the musical surface and the more tense the result.

Few composers pursue tempo proportions to such a state of abstraction. Great complication in one musical dimension inevitably leads to sacrifices in other dimensions. In the music in Figure 2, the extreme independence of the lines not only eliminates metrical depth but also weakens the sense of harmonic progression and phrasal articulation. But extreme solutions are often compelling and influential. Carter revealed new territory which subsequent composers explore as they wish.

A second influence is to some extent inseparable from the first: Carter's predilection for two or more kinds of music, or "characters," that unfold in overlapping and intricate patterns. It is said that he learned this kind of polyphonic discourse from Ives, just as his tempo schemes derive from Henry Cowell and Conlon Nancarrow; but he makes such influences his own. Some of the most exhilarating moments in Carter's music arise from overlaps of strongly contrasting musical characters— for instance, when the lower instruments begin to infiltrate the first-violin cadenza in the Second Quartet, beginning at bar 418.

A contrasting instance from the same work is the *Presto scherzando* second movement, in which the second violin marches on in obdurate pulsations while the other instruments scurry frantically in several directions. Just as Carter's tempi are strongly relational, so his musical characters are intensely social. In his music, individual behaviors are understood only in the context of other behaviors. Tempo is but one factor in forming characters: each character also carries its own melodic intervals, contour, and mood. Carter projects interacting personalities in lively and often conflicting conversations. The resulting music is vividly dramatic yet non-programmatic.

A third influence is for me the most powerful: Carter creates original forms that are integral to the musical materials yet intelligible in their overall shapes. In this respect he differs from two important modernist American composers with whom he is often associated, Roger Sessions and Milton Babbitt. Sessions, like Schoenberg in his 12-tone phase, tends to rely on formal schemas inherited from the German tonal tradition. To me (leaving aside other strengths in his music) this reliance is aesthetically problematic; sonata forms and the like belong to the musical syntax of the eighteenth and nineteenth centuries. Babbitt develops novel forms, but their effect is non-teleological and non-rhetorical. Partly for this reason, Babbitt's music often seems to exist in a perpetual, playful present, without beginning, middle, and end.

Carter, in contrast, has found formal means that arise from his methods of multiple tempi and interweaving characters. The driving force of the Second Quartet—despite its formal references to Allegro, Scherzo, Andante, and Finale—resides in the personalities of the individual instruments and their interaction through tempo proportions and polyphonic conversations. Their unfolding dramas carry the listener through the technical intricacies. The tentative gestures of the Introduction feel like a beginning, and its interruption by the first violin, at bar 35, conveys a second and more assertive beginning. The ending of the work is sensed already at the frantic climax of the fourth movement, bars 588-598; its resolution into the recollections of the Introduction in the dissipating Coda seems to follow inevitably. As listeners, we know where we are.

In later works, such as the Concerto for Orchestra and the Fifth Quartet, Carter dispenses with traditional formal references and freely creates intricate formal discourses that nevertheless remain intelligible.

A final influence is so general that it might better be called an ideal. Beginning with the Piano Sonata and Cello Sonata, all of Carter's music is instantly identifiable as his; yet he constantly renews himself, exploring new ideas with each piece. His output as a whole has a satisfying trajectory.

There is a coherent progression toward complexity from the Piano Sonata to the Double Concerto. After the immense complications of the Third Quartet, the music reverses yet progresses toward the comparative simplicity of the late period. A new lyricism emerges with *A Mirror on Which to Dwell* and subsequent vocal works. Carter's individual pieces take their place in one large work that is his life's work.

*****

Biography

Composer Fred Lerdahl studied at Lawrence University, Princeton, and Tanglewood. He has taught at UC/Berkeley, Harvard, and Michigan, and since 1991 he has been at Columbia University, where he is Fritz Reiner Professor of Music. He has received numerous honors for his music, including the Koussevitzky Composition Prize, two composer awards from the American Academy of Arts and Letters, and a Guggenheim Fellowship. Commissions have come from the Fromm Foundation, the Koussevitzky Foundation, the Spoleto Festival, the National Endowment for the Arts, the Chamber Music Society of Lincoln Center, the Library of Congress, and others. Among the organizations that have performed his works are the New York Philharmonic, the Pittsburgh Symphony, the San Francisco Symphony, the Seattle Symphony, the Cincinnati Symphony, the Los Angeles Philharmonic, the American Composers Orchestra, the Saint Paul Chamber Orchestra, the Orpheus Chamber Orchestra, the Manhattan Sinfonietta, the Boston Symphony Chamber Players, the Chamber Music Society of Lincoln Center, eighth blackbird, Speculum Musicae, Collage, Antares, the Juilliard Quartet, the Pro Arte Quartet, and the Venice Biennale. He has been in residence at the Marlboro Music Festival, IRCAM, the Wellesley Composers Conference, the American Academy in Rome, the Bowdoin Summer Music Festival, the Yellow Barn Music Festival, the Saint Paul Chamber Orchestra, and the Center for Advanced Study in the Behavioral Sciences. Lerdahl is also prominent as a music theorist. He has written two books, *A Generative Theory of Tonal Music* (with linguist Ray Jackendoff) and *Tonal Pitch Space*, both of which model musical listening from the perspective of cognitive science.

For the Winsor Music Consortium

Oboe Quartet

Fred Lerdahl
(2002)

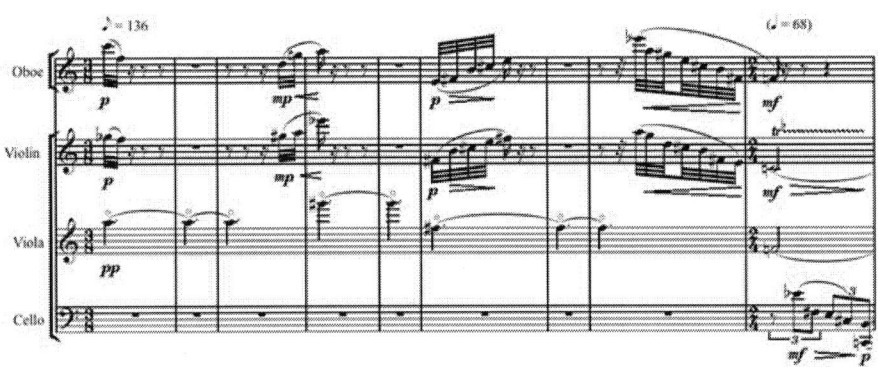

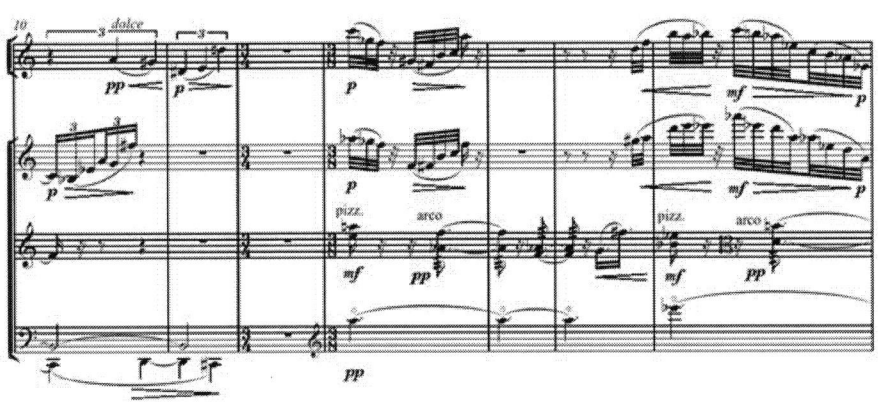

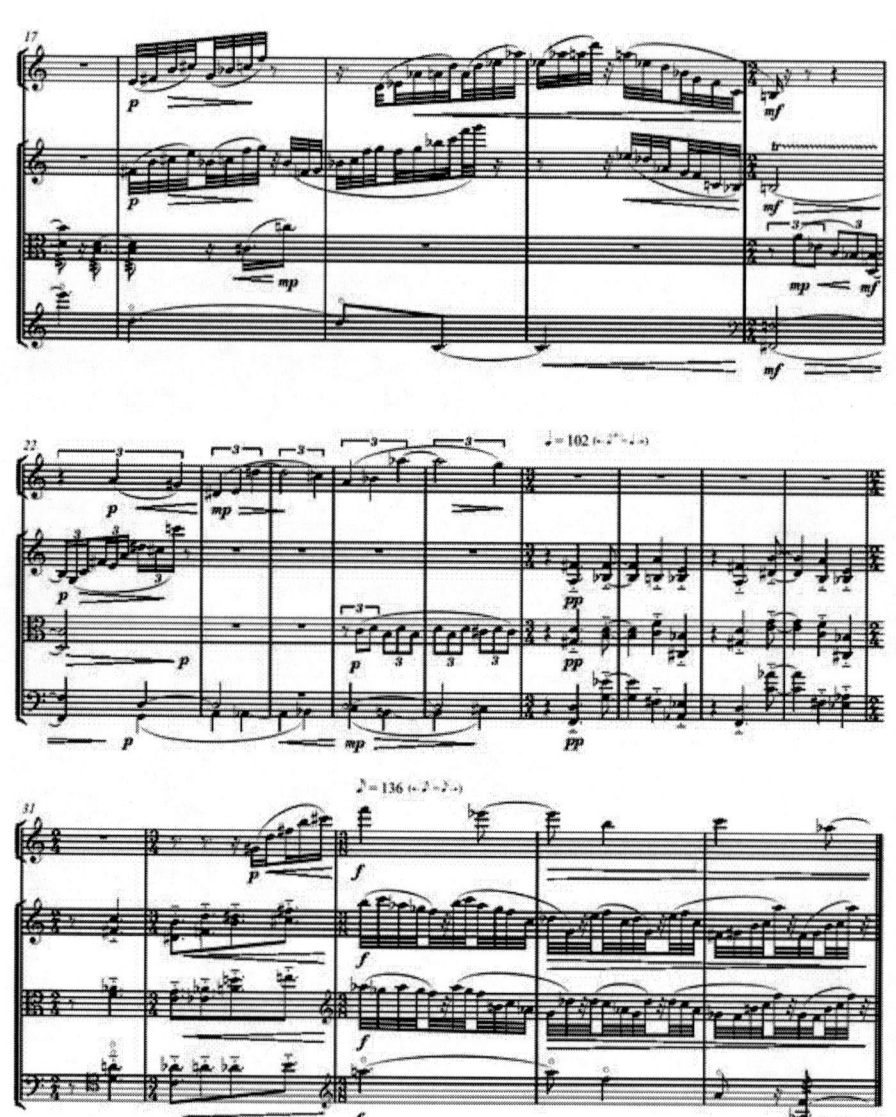

"Its full choir of echoes"

The composer in his library

Paul Griffiths

Elliott Carter, who breaks records in so many ways, must be among the most widely read of leading composers. In his youth, traveling to Europe regularly with his parents, he gained the beginnings of a familiarity with French, Italian and German, a familiarity he had many opportunities later to develop: Paris has been his second home since the time of his studies there with Nadia Boulanger (1932-5), and he has also spent long periods in Rome and Berlin. His knowledge of these countries' literatures, especially their poetic literatures, is extensive, while his deep conversance with literature in English goes back to his student days at Harvard. The Greek and Latin classics, too, he takes as part of his heritage, just as he takes Bach and Mozart as fundamental to the tradition within which he composes.

(A couple of personal observations may be pertinent here. While the libretto of *What Next?* was in progress, the composer, then nearing ninety, was rereading the *Aeneid* in Dryden's translation: a classic classicized. And one of the best stories ever told about Carter concerns a dinner party at which he was seated next to Aaron Copland. "What have you been reading?" Copland asked—evidently a regular question, which itself speaks of Carter's reputation. By now, though, Copland was in mental decline and put the question repeatedly, each time Carter answering with a little disquisition on a different book.)

Reading was there at the start, for Carter's life as a composer began, at least as far as the published record is concerned, with a ballet (*Pocahontas*) and a smattering of poetic settings, most of them choral, responding at once to his years in the Harvard Glee Club and to Boulanger's cultivation of Monteverdi. Two of the choral pieces set words by a poet inviting madrigalian treatment (Herrick), but the composer's trawl was wide:

Tarantella for men's choir and piano duet (1936): Ovid (43 B.C. – A.D. 17), from *Fasti*, set in the original and in Carter's translation

Harvest Home and **To Music** for choir (1937): Robert Herrick (1591-1674)

Let's be Gay for women's choir and piano (1937): John Gay (1685-1732), from *The Beggar's Opera*

Heart not so Heavy as Mine for choir (1938): Emily Dickinson (1830-86)

Tell me Where is Fancy Bred? for voice and guitar (1938): William Shakespeare (1564-1616), from *The Merchant of Venice*

The vocal works of Carter's thirties include some songs, but again many of the pieces are choral, if often larger in scale. One big difference is that now, apart from a setting from Urquart's Rabelais near the outset of this period, the composer preferred poets from his own country:

The Defense of Corinth for speaker, men's choir and piano duet (1941): François Rabelais (c.1494-1553), from *Pantagruel*, translated by Sir Thomas Urquart (1611-60)

Warble for Lilac-Time for high voice and chamber orchestra (1943): Walt Whitman (1819-92)

Three Poems for voice and piano (1943): Robert Frost (1874-1963)

Voyage for voice and piano (1943): Hart Crane (1899-1932)

The Harmony of Morning for women's choir and chamber orchestra (1944): Mark Van Doren (1894-1972)

Musicians Wrestle Everywhere for choir (1945): Dickinson

Emblems for men's choir and piano (1947): Allen Tate (1899-1979)

Then he stopped, and for more than a quarter of a century devoted himself to large-scale instrumental works. Some of these had images from poetry behind them: Lucretius's apostrophe to universal change in the Double Concerto of 1961, and, in the Concerto for Orchestra of 1968-9, the vision Saint-John Perse (1897-1975) described in his *Vents* of great winds sweeping the United States. Carter was similarly to disclose poetic images underlying subsequent works, including two he wrote for big orchestral resources: the Symphony of Three Orchestras of 1976-7 (Hart Crane again, *The Bridge*) and the *Symphonia* of 1993-7. The choice of subtext for this latter work could hardly be more Carterian: a Latin poem by an author belonging, like Herrick and Urquart, to the capaciously extravagant yet formal seventeenth century, *Bulla* (Bubble) by Richard Crashaw (c.1613-

49). But from the Cello Sonata 1948 to the violin-piano Duo and Brass Quintet of 1974 the human voice remained absent, and even seemed to have no possible place in music of such thrust and mercuriality.

Song's return came in 1975, in what turned out to be the first installment in a trilogy with ensemble accompaniment, followed at a distance by a cycle for the classic medium of voice and piano. As so long before, Carter chose U.S. poets, but this time poets of his own generation and younger.

A Mirror on Which to Dwell for soprano and ensemble (1975): Elizabeth Bishop (1911-79)

Syringa for mezzo-soprano, bass and ensemble (1978): John Ashbery (b. 1927) and ancient Gk.

In Sleep, in Thunder for tenor and ensemble (1981): Robert Lowell (1917-77)

Of Challenge and of Love for soprano and piano (1993): John Hollander (b. 1929)

Since his opera *What Next?* (1997-8) Carter has become once more a frequent songster, as he was sixty or seventy years before, and again more various in what he sets. There are songs in Italian and French, and two further cycles looking back to poets who, like Hart Crane, Mark Van Doren and Allen Tate in former times, would have been eagerly read by Harvard students of Carter's generation.

Tempo e tempi for soprano and four players (1998-9): Eugenio Montale (1896-1981), Salvatore Quasimodo (1901-68) and Giuseppe Ungaretti (1888-1970)

Of Rewaking for mezzo-soprano and orchestra (2002): William Carlos Williams (1883-1963)

In the Distances of Sleep for mezzo-soprano and ensemble (2005-6): Wallace Stevens (1879-1955)

Mad Regales for six voices (2007): Ashbery

La Musique for mezzo-soprano (2007): Charles Baudelaire (1821-67)

In that respect Carter's tour of his library is circular, at least in its focus. A lot, though, has changed. When Carter came back to vocal writing in 1975, he was master of a musical world he had developed with other prospects in view. His response—bold at what then seemed the rather advanced age of sixty-six—was to reinvent that world around the voice, or, rather, from out of the voice, as if singing, so long excluded, had become central, even germinal.

When the Bishop-Lowell-Ashbery trilogy was completed, even Carter's instruments began to sing, first in his Triple Duo (1982-3), which is lighter and more humorous than his earlier chamber works, and then in a succession of small-scale instrumental inventions that began in 1984 with *Riconoscenza per Goffredo Petrassi* for violin and *Esprit rude/Esprit doux* for flute and clarinet, and that has continued unabated. The composer also started writing for singing instruments in his concertos: oboe, violin, clarinet, cello and, most recently, horn. A comparison of his Fourth Quartet (1985) with his Third (1971) might be enough to show the revolution in his linear thinking that could be ascribed to his reintroduction of the voice.

But if the voice changed his music, his music also changed the voice, changed singing. The vocal personae that sing out of Carter's post-1975 music are very little like those of his earlier songs. Nor are they much like those of any other music, with the possible exception of Stravinsky's late settings, such as the Three Shakespeare Songs and *Elegy for J.F.K.*—works composed while Carter was vocally silent.

One could characterize the voice's role in most western vocal music as that of deliverer: the music creates the impression of a personality, which seems to be conveying a message. In late Carter and late Stravinsky, however, there is no such distinction between personality (stable, even while able to express a wide range of meanings and nuances) and message. The personality is flickering, uncertain. Nor does it seem that the message is responsible, as it might be in the expression of extreme emotion. The delivery is subject to other forces—forces that are, perhaps, not entirely outside the enunciating voice, forces of disruption that belong to it, or at least pertain to it, and work against any understanding of it as a conscious, singular entity. Music's ability to create a personality for its own conveyance is destabilized. Song springs from out of a nowhere, a no-one, or possibly from out of an interconnecting but by no means homogeneous choir. There is no single authority, no single authentic source.

The ungroundedness of the Carterian voice is partly, and maybe most patently, a matter of a characteristic mismatching of metre between the vocal line and its accompaniment. *Of Challenge and of Love* provides clear examples, as in the middle song, "Am Klavier" (At the Piano), where the eponymous instrument maintains a more or less consistent pulse every five triplet sixteenth-notes against the voice's looser eighth-note regime— a ratio of pulse rates between voice and piano of 5: 3.

But Carter goes further than this in keeping the elements separate. The voice and the piano would have an opportunity to coincide every two and a half quarter-notes, this duration representing three pulses for the piano and five for the voice. However, the composer allows this to happen only once in the entire song. Of course, this exceptional moment is significant. It comes on the word "pluck," about two-thirds of the way through, where the singer's C sharp (her lowest note in this song) is doubled by the piano, which adds the E immediately above. The gesture—accented in the voice, staccato in the piano—is onomatopoeic. Voice and piano are conjoined just twice more, outside the grid of pulses every five triplet sixteenth-notes. The first of these occurrences comes on a word with a long history of emphasis in song: "love," as it arrives in the phrase Carter took as his title. Here the voice's D sharp is again doubled in the accompaniment, with the warm support of an augmented triad. Finally, the first word of the concluding phrase, "like a kind of light," is also sung together with the piano, but this time without doubling of notes. The piano's backing here seems to provide a gentle prop against which this last line can lift off.

Except in these cases, the voice's attacks are sprinkled among those of the piano, which has the practical advantage of helping the singer project her notes and her words, even as it leaves her without the rhythmic scaffolding of a more conventional accompaniment. The two participants' togetherness is reconfigured. They are on their own, metrically, and yet their separatenesses are interdependent. If rhythmic coincidence is infrequent, the common alertness, of each to the other, must be no less acute. On a more poetic plane, the absence of a single pulse contributes markedly to the absence of a single persona. Vocal expression is not governing the musical flow—or, rather, the musical flows, for they are several.

The most conspicuous beat comes from the piano, with its pulsations every five triplet sixteenth-notes, slowing to every ten in large parts of the song. This time-measuring is most audible—because constant and relatively free from the chords and additional figuration that often filter into the piano part—in parts of the song printed below in Roman type; its repetitions are halved in frequency where the underlining falls away:

<u>The evening light dies down: all the old songs begin</u>
<u>To crowd the soft air, choiring confusedly.</u>
<u>Then above that sea of *immense complexities*</u>

The clear tenor of memory I did not know
I had enters; like a rod of text held out by
A god of meaning, it governs the high, wayward
Waves of what is always going on in the world.
All that becomes accompaniment. And it is
What we start out with now: this is no time
To pluck or harp on antiquities of feeling.
These *soft hammers give gentle blows to all their strings,*
Blows that strike with a touch of challenge and of love.
Thus what we are, being sung against what we come
To be part of, *rises like* a *kind of light.*

Roughly the same process is happening three times over here, with increasing speed: the regular pulse first falls out of immediate earshot because other material intervenes in the piano, then that pulse misses alternate beats. First time round, the piano starts moving toward "immense complexities" with (usually) two-note chords off the basic pulse, as it had briefly before the voice entered. The piano returns to its faster pulsations, and overtly so, at the momentous words "this is no time," occurring in what would, if this were a normal sort of sonnet, be the first line of the sestet. (This is also the only line in which Hollander's pentameters become orthodoxly iambic.) At this point the additional material is contributed by eighth-note pulses, drawing particular attention to the piano's gentle hammer blows, these pulses being displaced from the vocal line by a sixteenth-note so as, once more, to avoid coincidences. Finally, as the voice slows toward the close, the piano's pattern returns, and disappears.

To interpret this process on, again, a more poetic level, the piano's regular pulsation, coming almost every second (the tempo indication is quarter-note=c.76, which would mean a pulse rate of c.63 for five triplet sixteenth-notes), might represent clock time—not now governing events, as pulsation does in conventionally metrical music, but there among those events, like a clock in a dream. This pulsation is submerged within the confused choiring of old songs, but it goes steadily on, at second or two-second intervals, and might be understood as the unknown memory trace, "like a rod of text," which governs (certainly it underpins) the high, wayward waves of what is always going on in this song. It resurfaces at the mention of time, and again at the mention of what we are, for what we are is perhaps to be interpreted as this choiring of times: the objective and given (pulsation) with the subjective and acquired.

Also to be considered are the varieties of time through which the voice moves in its progress through the song. Four different speeds of enunciation can be distinguished, with average note lengths of around two sixteenth notes, three (the usual), four to five and seven. The resulting changes of effective tempo are represented by changes of spacing in the text that follows:

> The evening light dies down: all the old songs begin
>
> To crowd the soft air, choiring confusedly.
>
> Then above that sea of immense complexities
>
> T h e c l e a r t e n o r o f memory I did not know
>
> I had enters; like a rod of text held out by
>
> A god of meaning, it governs the high, wayward
>
> Waves of what is always going on in the world.
>
> Allthatbecomesaccompoaniment.Anditis
>
> What we start out with now: this is no time
>
> To pluck or harp on antiquities of feeling.
>
> These soft hammers give gentle blows to all their strings,
>
> Blows that strike with a touch of challenge and of love.
>
> Thus what we are, being sung against what we come
>
> To be part of, r i s e s   l i k e   a   k i n d   o f   l i g h t .

The fastest speed is reserved for the eighth line, and the jitteriness there is intensified by staccato enunciation, suited to words made largely of short syllables. This kind of setting is echoed, but nearer the song's default speed, at the words "against what we come to be part of," which recall the eighth line in sound and meaning. As for the slowest speed, that comes just at the end, where the song is decelerating—and, in the piano, thinning—as it rises to the light. There is more frequent intervention from the intermediately slower music, whose appearances partly accord with—and partly modify—changes in the pulsation layer marked in the previous quotation of the text. Thus, for example, the prominence given "the clear tenor" comes just after the pulsations have fallen into the background, and the slower speed returns as they do in the ninth line and the thirteenth. The emphasis on the word "love" requires no explanation, any more than do the similar emphases on "god," "world" and "time"—all relatively high notes approached through intervals of a fifth ("a god" and "no time" are both set to C-G; "of love" is another fifth, a minor third down) or minor sixth ("the world").

With melodic aspects of the setting thus introduced, one might observe how most of the song is confined to the diminished octave from E up to E flat. The singer has got as far as "I," at the beginning of the fifth line, before she dips below, to C sharp, and as far as "god," in the next line, before she rises above her habitual range, to G. And these, apart from a lone A flat near the end, are the limits. In a cycle that moves from low A sharp to high B at the climax of its fourth song, "Am Klavier" avoids the extremes, and ventures outside its usual confines only on rare occasions, marked below by bold type for low notes and italic for high. Also shown here, in upper-case type, are places where the melody repeats a note that has appeared before with from one to four notes in between:

> the evening light dies down: ALL the old songs begin
> TO crowd the soft air, choiring CONfusedly.
> then above that SEA of IMmense COMplexities
> THE clear tenor of memorY i DID NOT know
> i hAD enters; like A rod of text HELD out BY
> a *god* of meaning, IT GO*V*ERNS the high, WAYward
> waves OF what is a*l*WAYS GOING ON in the *world*.
> ALL that becomes accompaNIment. AND it IS
> WHAT WE START out WITH now: this *is* no *time*
> to **pluck** OR HARP on **ANTIQUITIES** OF feeling.
> these so**FT** hammers give gentle **blows** TO **ALL** their strings,
> **BLOWS** that STRIKE WITH a touch OF challenge and of love.
> *thus* WHAT we are, BEING *sung* aGAINST what WE *COME*
> TO BE part of, *ri*sES like A kind of light.

These matters of note placement exert themselves toward ends both formal and expressive. All the low notes, apart from the first, are in lines 10-12, all the high notes outside this region, in lines 6-7, 9 and 13-14. The song first establishes its home range, then touches new extremes (lines 5-6), keeps returning to the high G or F sharp (lines 6-9), plumbs the low C sharp ("pluck...an[tiqui]ties") and E flat/D sharp ("so[ft]...blows...all...blows"), and, in the last two lines, visits a new set of high notes: F, E and A flat. Then again, as with the long durations, the exceptional pitches often serve to emphasize key words. The percussive "pluck" has already been noted; one might observe also the repercussions that follow, suggestive of repeated hammer blows, or the use of high notes to draw attention ("thus" at the start of the final couplet) or illustrate. The word "sung," for example, expresses itself in a high melisma (E - A flat - F), which stands out not only by reason of register but also by its nature in a setting that is otherwise almost entirely syllabic, the only other exceptions being the two-note straddles for "soft" (both times it appears), "had" (line 5) and "are" (line 13).

As for places where notes are quickly (but not immediately) repeated, these also stand out, especially where a group of them is concerned: "memory I did not...it governs...always going on...what we start out with...or harp on antiquities of...blows that strike with...being sung against what we come to be." Here the context is important. The first song of the cycle has very little such repetition; the second is full of it, being an echo song. Now the echoes are fewer, and come not only in response to the poem's assonance and alliteration ("crowd the soft air, choiring confusedly," "wayward waves," etc.)—not a direct response, of course; rather a musical parallel that runs through the song from the fourth line on—but also in answer to the key themes of memory and re-sounding (as, indeed, the assonances and alliterations do). It is the mention of memory that triggers the first wobble of note repetitions, and though the metaphor does not hold fast—the same kind of gesture can be used for mundane routine ("what is always going on in the world") and "antiquities of feeling"—it is also this clear, unknown memory that "is what we start out with now" and that is forming "what we come to be part of." Or perhaps the oscillation—between stretches where notes revolve and others where the norm is a succession of six or seven different pitches—is to be understood as a continuous condition in which memory and movement, reflection and change are embedded in one another, a condition in which past and present are simultaneous.

One might find that condition, too, in how the vocal line trembles with echoes not only from within itself but also out of further musical pasts. The basic seven-note set (F sharp - D - C - E - G - A flat - D flat as it appears in the piano introduction, reading upwards in register) can give rise to various kinds of scalar or triadic entity, instances starting with the setting of the opening words (E - G - A - B - G) and of "soft air" (E flat - A flat - C). Of course, these shadows are faint and transitory—except in the startling case of the augmented triad under the word "love," where the piano's chord is even repeated in the voice as a descending line at "what we are." Interpretation of this striking moment, however, has to be uncertain, in ways and for reasons that are characteristic not only of this song but of Carter's music as a whole. Much has been said already of the entanglement of formal with expressive meanings. So it is here. The setting of "what we are" has to be read as a direct reference back to the "love" chord, which will still be echoing in the listener's (and indeed the singer's) memory, having been struck only seven quarter-notes earlier, but does the reference work in terms of meaning (what we are comes from love, or urges toward it) or of rhetoric? It comes, after all, as a strong echo among a variety of weaker ones, and a turning point that confirms, after the high F on "Thus," the arrival into the song's last two lines.

There are, then, several layers of activity through which the song proceeds, insisting on its character not as a declaration from a persona but rather as something that is, through the one voice, projecting a choir. The internal clock comes forward and recedes; the speed alters; exceptions occur below or above the central vocal texture; notes reverberate within the line; glimmerings of other musical worlds appear. In each of these ways the song avoids stability, becomes choric in every dimension, while the various dimensions together produce multiple effects of mutual support and contradiction. Rather than projecting a meaning, the song seems to be going in search of meaning, testing itself right up to its ultimate dissolution.

Yet perhaps this atmosphere of self-questioning is created most of all—more than by the voice's instabilities—by the interweaving of voice and piano. Just as the voice keeps to the middle of its range so does the piano. The right hand reaches beyond the voice's furthest limit (A flat) only very occasionally—furthest and most emphatically at the crux already noted in other areas, where the turn comes to the last couplet. Once again, the confinement has a practical advantage, in allowing the voice prominence (though this by no means stops Carter using the upper treble in the other songs of the cycle), while at the same time it enhances the integration of voice and piano. As for the left hand, the part rarely slips below the bass staff, and much of the music unfolds within a space of not much more than two octaves. This registral frame is tightened further in the central part of the song, from "always going on" to "antiquities of feeling," where everything in the piano is contained between the B below the treble staff and the A above, a range only just exceeding the voice's. Apart from anything else, this points up the move to a lower and somewhat wider span, from the D below the bass staff to the A sharp above, for the section from "These soft hammers" to immediately before the climactic word "love," where the effect of the augmented triad is heightened by its appearing as light after gloom, a gloom surely evocative of the piano's felted percussions. After this return of the treble—and briefly the upper treble, as already mentioned—the piano settles back into the ambit it had at the start.

Through all these changes there is a continuity. Since the vocal tessitura is also lowest where the piano's is, the two can imitate one another, and indeed they do so right through the song, the piano providing a persistent texture of echoes and pre-echoes on the immediate plane of realized sound. It is as if the two are engaged in a slippery canon, where it is impossible to say which is leading and which following; there is just always the tremble of reverberations. Thus what we are is sung against what we come to be a part of, as through and within the chiming-singing of these two voices together we hear the braided songs of a choir.

* * * * *

Biography

Paul Griffiths was born in Bridgend, Wales, in 1947. He studied biochemistry at Oxford, and began writing music criticism professionally in 1971, gaining staff posts on *The Times* of London (1979-92) and *The New Yorker* (1992-6). His first book, *A Concise History of Modern Music*, came out in 1978, and has been translated into several languages, including French, Dutch, Japanese, Portuguese, and Welsh. Among his other books on music are *The Sea on Fire* (a biography of Jean Barraqu•), *The Penguin Companion to Classical Music*, *The Substance of Things Heard* (selected reviews and essays), and *A Concise History of Western Music*. His first novel, *Myself and Marco Polo*, won the Commonwealth Writer's Prize in 1989, and he has written words for music by Mozart (*The Jewel Box*) and Beethoven (*The General*), as well as Elliott Carter (*What Next?*). He has given lectures and courses on various musical topics, invited by institutions ranging from the Munich Biennale to Harvard. In 2002 he was honored by the French government as a Chevalier de l'Ordre des Arts et des Lettres. He lives in Manorbier, Wales, with his wife, and has two sons.

Of Challenge and of Love, copyright 1995 Hendon Music, Inc., a Boosey & Hawkes company. Copyright for all countries. All rights reserved. Reprinted by permission.

"ITS FULL CHOIR OF ECHOES"

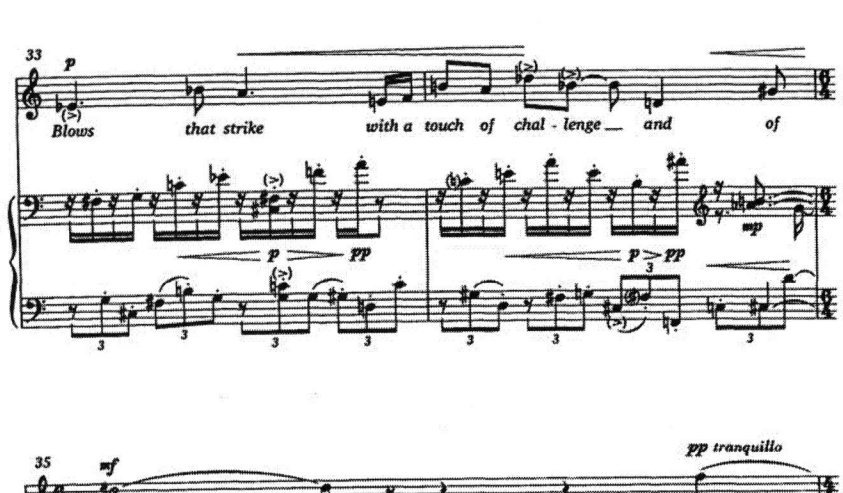
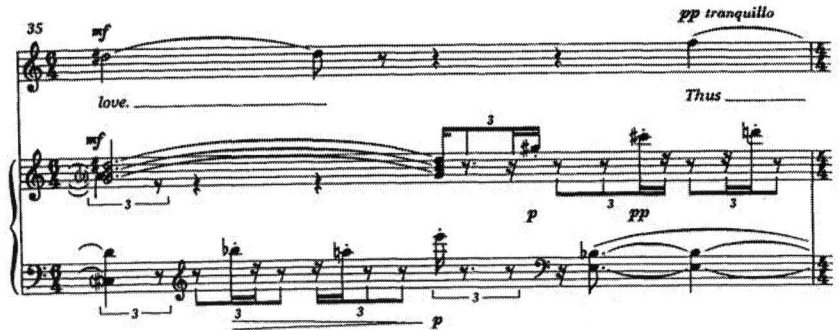
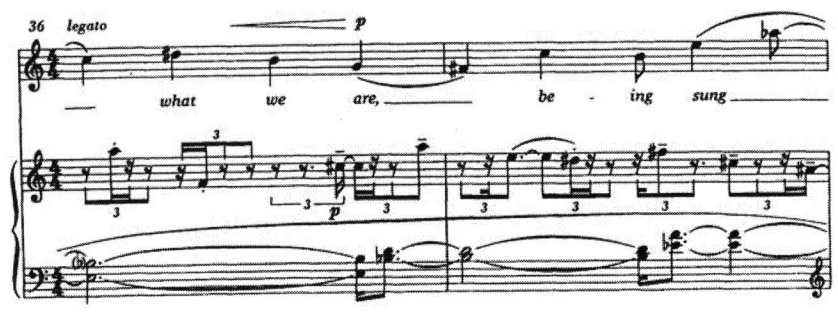

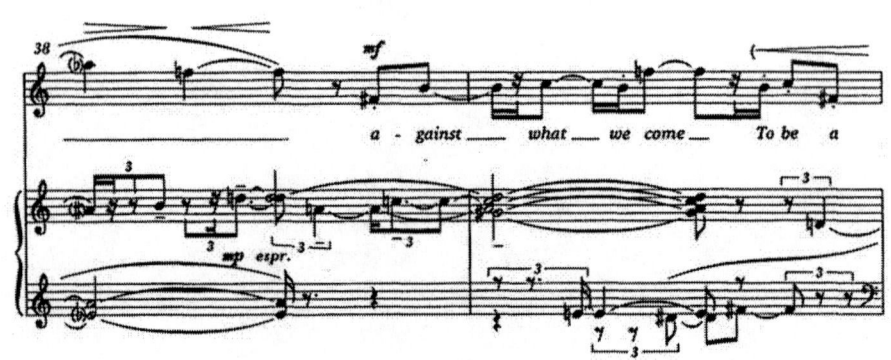
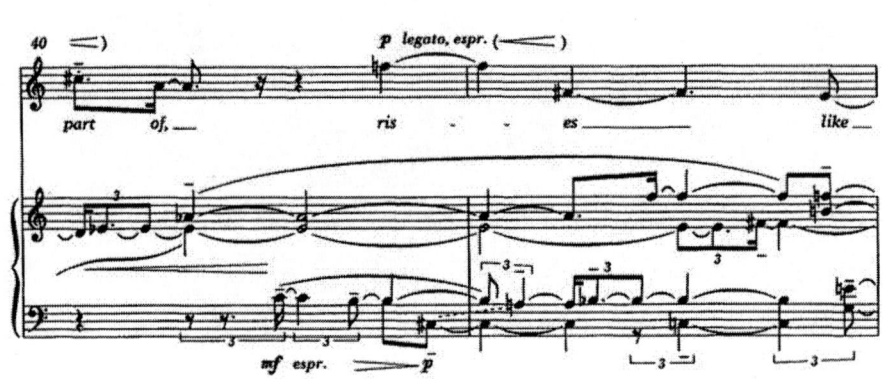
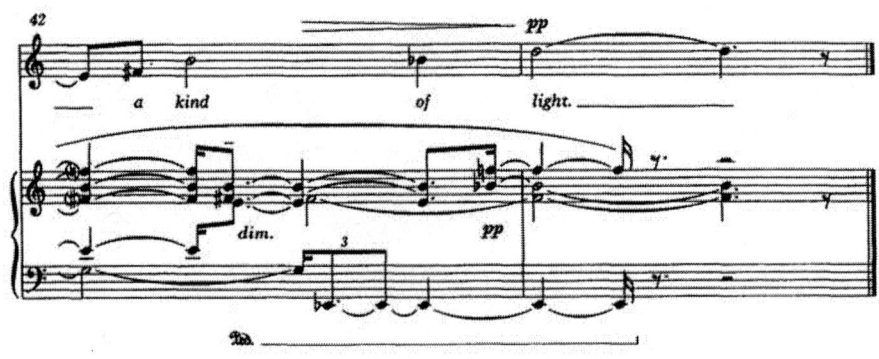

"e poi…"

Alvin Curran

As a devoted purveyor of chords I felt my heart beat wildly when in 2005, after some searching, I found a copy of Elliott Carter's *Harmony Book* in the Lincoln Center Music shop. I thought as I opened it, as I'd thought starting all the books on Harmony I'd devoured since I was nine years old, that I would be given the keys to some magic universe, beyond Harry Potter's wizardry, where music could be made understandable, legal, accessible, physical and transparent, even modern, wondrous, and above all composable. No book on Harmony, except Elliott's, has ever done this. His Harmony book is the Rosetta Stone of the Music of our Time—as perfectly decipherable as it is indecipherable. Perfectly chiseled in an ancient mysterious script, it is in reality a meticulous systematic catalogue of every possible combination of tones in the almighty equal tempered West; and brilliantly, shockingly, lacking any "instructions for use." His music, following his obsessive skill in codifying intervallic relations (and their sonic potential), is a realization of their finite combinatorial possibilities. But unlike the rigid and impersonal relations long touted by 12-tone theorist-composers, the tonal and temporal intervals of Elliott's "mind music" are meant to translate "subito" into meaningful sounds, gestures, structures, parables, and even emotions—akin to the analytic foundations which lie under much of Xenakis's, Ligeti's, Stockhausen's, Tom Johnson's, and even Cage's music. Elliott's *Harmony Book* is in effect the "inner sanctum" of his composing world, though just short of telling you how he puts it all together it leaves the reader to make those imaginary leaps of faith, as do Cage's late number pieces. It is as close to a composer's confession of how (with what) he composes as one can get.

    I can well remember the imposing smell of mold (composted music?) in Yale's old Stoeckel Hall in New Haven where, on a warm September Friday in 1960, I met Elliott for the first time. In a small room on the top floor were Tom Johnson, Joel Chadabe, David Barron, me, and two other students whose names I've forgotten. We sat in awe, awaiting God knows what—to burst into composerly flames maybe—but all we got was a mild mannered gentleman in a tweed jacket, blue striped shirt, and tie. Elliott was as new at "teaching composition" as we were at studying it as a life's career. He was aware that we were all hot to learn the secrets of "metric modulation" and the rest of those journalistic buzz words that kept ordinary concert-goers wondering why anyone would want to write music like that... not just like Elliott's but the whole Princeton Columbia world's, not to mention the music of heretics like Partch, Lou Harrison, Nancarrow, and Cage.

Elliott forewarned us against trying to imitate his music—which in those early days—before the "new complexity" thing—was an understandable concern. None of us did, back then it was inimitable! At the same time he let us know clearly that he could field anything, any music in any modernist language, as long as it had no octaves. Octaves were not admissible in that room, or as far as Elliott was concerned anywhere beyond the 19th century (with special dispensation for Stravinsky). In the two years that I met with Elliott every Friday of the school calendar, I felt I was somehow becoming a composer—a dream that had been begging for some time to become reality. I cannot say how this happened, but I feel that Elliott's generous caring toward us and his unquestioned commitment to the "profession" were precious lessons in themselves, along with the dogged attention to detail that he gave equally to all his students: he urged us to find refined ways of questioning everything and even more refined ways of reshaping linear contours, of molding the flow and density of sonic mass, of avoiding banal literal repetition when a subtle variant could be created, of scrutinizing register, orchestration, and overall intention. Elliott, I realized long after I graduated, had simply treated us, his first students, like young professionals—without our knowing it he had admitted us to the inner circle where the pros sat, ate lunch, drank, and talked shop. I quickly devoured all of Elliott's available music, finding special inspirational affinity with the *Piano Sonata* (1946). While that work and the related *Sonata for Cello and Piano* (1948) did presage the "real" Elliott Carter that followed—the Carter of pure structure as pure sound, as in the *First String Quartet*—those later pieces demanded I revise my ideas about all music (few as they were then) and that was hard, almost impossible.

On the other hand, we had the privilege of working with Elliott at a moment when his own career was taking off in a big way. The *Second String Quartet*, a model of ordered madness—the players confined to polyphonic temporal isolation rooms—which for the life of me I could never quite grasp, was in the works (today it's a lovable piece of cake). So was the *Double Concerto for Piano Harpsichord and Percussion*—an inspired work of sonic problem solving, which even under the alcohol-dipped baton of the great Bruno Maderna became a wonder to hear, as I did in Berlin in

1964. Both of these pieces incidentally are founded on simple and effective ideas of spatialization which became one of my own prominent compositional themes. Unlike so many dedicated academic teachers in American universities, Elliott was actually a composer in the real world, and this made an enormous impression on me and my colleagues –Elliott was already there, "out there."

After Yale Graduate School I was well on my chosen path, and I turned down a Fulbright that would have let me study with Berio, in order to accompany Elliott when he invited me to Berlin in 1964, along with Joel Chadabe and Frederic Rzewski, to be a "young composer" in the first year of the DAAD program—then under the auspices of the Ford Foundation. In addition to other joys of those times, which I have written about often, I became a friend of Helen and Elliott's which has been for me a lifelong blessing. Those who know my music and its maverick character will know it has little to do with the world that Elliott would have liked me to be a part of. At the same time, there is not a thing I write that I do not put under some kind of Carteresque scrutiny.... even the Octaves, even the triads, even the clusters—even the sampled loons on my Powerbook.

Once Elliott's music abandoned its early roots in the populist American tradition, it became and has remained a shining model of what one might call gentlemanly experimentalism, music which questioned everything except the major institutions for which it was destined—its relentless sound as disconcerting as the Partches' and the Cages' and the Musica Elettronica Vivas' in its endless research into new musical realms. A big difference lay in its regal demands for the very best performers, the best rehearsal schedules, the best halls and the best of a curious and informed public. There are no detectable concessions to anything or anyone in Elliott's work, and this makes him a maverick of a very special kind, one for whom the modernist utopia of societal education and transformation and art for art remains forever a viable goal despite the wobbly economics of today's symphony orchestras and the philosophy of do-it-yourself mayhem espoused by many of us born after him. While I do not myself compose with a narrative sensibility (relying neither on the Greeks nor the moderns for cues) I do feel that my dogged music of old fashioned instinct is in some way related to the tradition of great composing and the refined experimentalism whose essence is Elliott. Our mutual respect and friendship has only grown over the years, and now with Elliott in his 100th year I am happy to write these words, wishing only that Helen were here to read them too.

ELLIOTT CARTER
E Poi

Alvin Curran

* play this section quietly but tending toward mp- even mf as speed and density changes suggest.

"E POI…"

* * * * *

Biography

Alvin Curran, a persistent innovator in today's new music world, brings the whole environment into unpredictable focus through his sonic fireworks, sharp wit, and timeless lyricism. He co-founded the legendary improvising ensemble Musica Eletronica Viva in 1965 with Frederic Rzewski and Richard Teitelbaum, and in the early 70s began creating a poetic series of solo-performance works for synthesizer, voice, taped environmental sounds and found objects. In seeking out new musical spaces in the late 70's he began to develop a series of concert events to be given on lakes, in ports, parks, buildings, quarries and extended to include whole countries in simultaneous radio concerts with live musicians in multiple countries, and evolving into large scale musical choreographic works such as OH BRASS ON THE GRASS ALAS, for 300 amateur brass-band musicians, which opened the 2006 Donaueschingen Festival, and MARITIME RITES TATE, performed by 200 musicians including members of the London Symphony Orchestra Brass Ensemble on and around the Thames River in September 2007.

Curran taught at the National Academy of Dramatic Arts in Rome, Italy, was Darius Milhaud Professor of Composition at Mills College between 1992 and 2006, and continues to teach privately in Rome. He has published many articles on musical topics, including at the New York Times website, and has received awards from BMI, the National Endowment for the Arts, DAAD, Ars Acoustica, Prix Italia, Premio Novecento, Fromm Foundation, the Hass Family, Leonardo Award for Excellence, Ars Electronica, Phonurgia Nova, the Guggenheim Foundation; he has been interviewed by the Yale Oral History American Music project.

On Elliott Carter's "Anaphora," from *A Mirror on Which to Dwell*[1]

Louis Karchin

Although I have heard the work in concert several times, my first encounter with the score of Elliott Carter's eloquent settings of Elizabeth Bishop's poetry occurs at an odd moment. It is months before I am scheduled to conduct this piece, but I find myself with score in hand and a free hour on the opening summer day of Boston University's Tanglewood Institute for high school students. My daughter, Marisa, is entering the Young Artist Vocal Program, and my wife and daughter are putting the final touches on her dorm room, which now appears to contain a significant proportion of the contents of our house. However, when I travel, I also take music with me to study, since I find composing—my primary activity—impossible to do away from home. With some time to spare now, sitting on the lawn outside BUTI's Groton Hall, I open up the *Mirror* for the first time.

A conductor tends to worry about practicalities at the outset. How difficult will this be for the musicians? For the conductor? What will the rehearsal issues be? The opening of the first song is a wash of color—winds, strings, vibraphone and piano all playing rapid, wildly-leaping arpeggios. The instruments subdivide the basic quarter-note beat into either 4 or 5 units. But it's the pitches that attract my attention. There seems to be an anchoring note—either D or B depending on where you look—and infinite variety above these roots. On closer inspection, many pitches seem "fixed" in particular registers, the most important being F, F sharp, C, G, and B flat (in ascending order above the bass notes). As I imagine the music in my head, I realize why I am favoring D as the root of this chord: I am simultaneously listening to a brass section rehearsing the last movement of Sibelius' Second Symphony. A group of students have remarkably convened even before registration to get a jump on the challenges of the summer. The Sibelius movement is in the key of D, and the part to which I am listening is the second theme, a majestic but repetitive idea which slowly builds in intensity.

I turn my attention back to the *Mirror*. Looking further through the instrumental part of the first song, "Anaphora," I notice that the D and B

A Mirror in Which to Dwell by Elliott Carter and Elizabeth Bishop. Copyright 1976 (Renewed by Associated Music Publishers, Inc (BMI). International Copyright Secured. All Rights Reserved. Used by Permission

ON ELLIOTT CARTER'S "ANAPHORA"

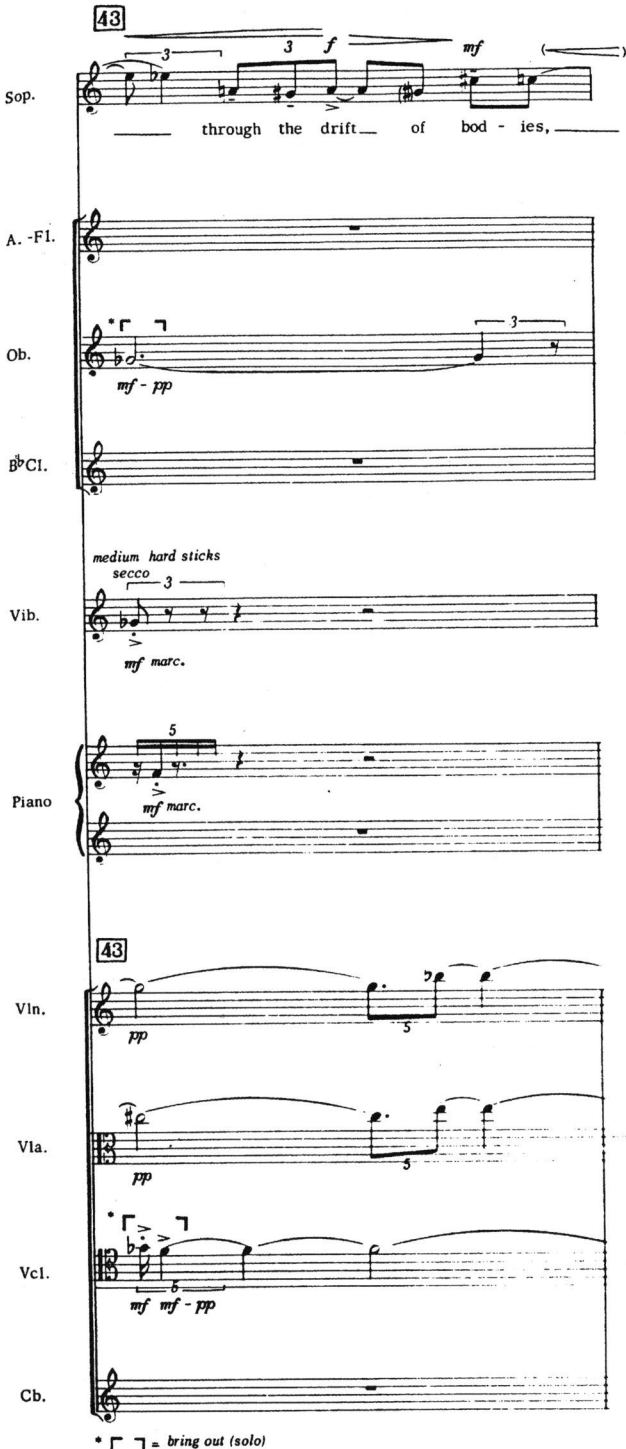

ELLIOTT CARTER

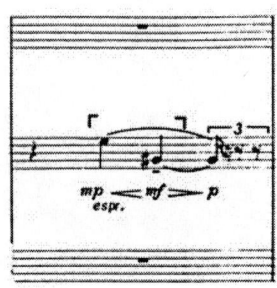

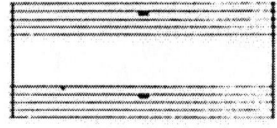

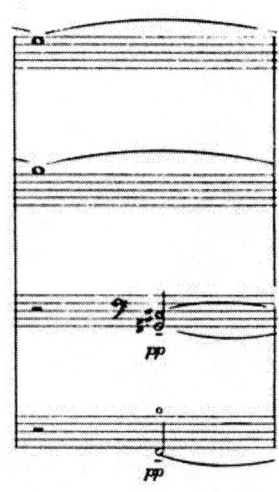

roots seldom leave, and the energy is relentless until measure 22, where the mood changes markedly. Notes still seem fixed in the registers noted above. I glance at the text—there is nothing in it that would necessarily mandate such an approach. I notice the poem's title, which implies a repetitive literary device, but the poet herself has made use of repetition only in three small instances: the words, "mortal, "instantly" and "endless" are stated twice in succession as they appear. I continue paging through the remainder of the movement. Although the roots of the chords disappear from time to time as the music becomes less frenetic, they are, at the very least, always implied if not boldly stated. The pitches above them are still fixed in place. I check the date of the work; maybe I am discovering some unlikely minimalist influence on Carter that no one has yet detected. It was written in 1975 though, and it occurs to me that any influence is more likely to have come from a work such as Boulez's first *Improvisation sur Mallarmé*, a score also predisposed towards fixed pitch registration. I become aware again of the Sibelius, still in the background, and it is a reminder that composers have always been fascinated with repetitive devices.

My mind begins to wander and I remember my very first meeting with Elliott Carter only a few years before he composed the *Mirror*, in the summer of 1972. The place was less than a mile from where I am now sitting. I was a twenty year-old aspiring composer, in the Fellowship program of the Tanglewood Music Center, and Carter was a senior guest composer that summer. Over the course of several weeks, he met with the eight or so Composition Fellows, always at the Hawthorne Cottage just on the edge of the Tanglewood grounds. I remember the enormous respect he engendered among us, and also his easy-going manner. Carter brought with him a recording of his *Concerto for Orchestra*, a recent work which had garnered immense acclaim. He seemed genuinely pleased with it, but not at all in an egocentric way. He spoke of it as if he was as amazed as anyone that he had written it, and thankful that it had turned out as he had hoped. He was eager to share it with us. He talked a good bit about some of his compositional preoccupations over the years: metric modulation, and his practice of assigning certain intervals as primary ones to particular instruments. What I remember most though, were the vivid pictures that seemed to help him crystallize musical ideas. "This is the place where the machine eats the man," I remember him saying at one point, in reference to a particularly rambunctious moment. He stressed that we should look for compositional procedures that would help us write the music already within us. He had experimented with serialism at one time, he said, but mostly, he wanted to do "a little of this and a little bit of that," and serialism, for him, had not been enough of a spring-board for the continual variety that he had been seeking.

One day, one of us got up enough courage to ask him something about which we were all curious. "In the very complex sections of your music—for example the climax of the Second String Quartet—can you hear everything?" There was a short pause, but it turned out Carter was not at all offended by the question. "Probably not every single note," I recall him saying. "But generally, yes, and I would definitely know if something were wrong." This answer seemed to satisfy everyone. After all, we reasoned, in tonal music, you cannot hear everything either. You may think that you do, but can your inner ear really capture every element of figuration in a very complex Rimsky-Korsakov or Debussy orchestration? Probably not. We debated this for several days among ourselves.

I look at my watch and I have been day-dreaming for some time now. The brass section has moved on to Stravinsky's *Firebird*. I go back to my original intention and begin looking through the first song for performance problems. There is an easy metric modulation near the beginning, but then Carter begins to subdivide the new 6/8 time in several ways: some groups of instruments divide the dotted quarter-note beat into three parts, some into two or four. The tempo is slow enough and the texture active enough so that the musicians would need to think in terms of the subdivisions, but as a conductor, I might be able to conduct in dotted quarters—thus contradicting neither group. Carter seems to have calculated the tempo perfectly: the music is slow enough to highlight the different subdivisions of the beat, but fast enough to allow the dotted quarter-note pulse to act as a unifying element. I notice that instruments tend to play on downbeats, which will help with overall coordination. Then I spot measure 5, where the violinist must come in just after the beat, play rapidly, utilizing the four-part subdivision against the three, and land just before the next downbeat, but not on it. I try to picture ways in which our violinist, Curtis Macomber, might do this. Finally I realize it is not so difficult because no one else is playing a counter-rhythm against him in this particular measure. This reminds me of other "difficult" spots I have encountered in Carter's music. He pushes players to their limits, especially rhythmically, but seems to know where to draw a final boundary. I remember that Carter told us in his seminars that he wanted his music to be fun to perform. When we asked him about specific pitch choices, he referred back to this comment saying that the process of making the gestures "fun" even influenced the pitch choices themselves. I think his attitude towards performance practice has always been a rather traditional one—that the composer might write complicated music, but he should nonetheless help the performer as much as possible to execute the work with fluidity, so that it might "sound" easy. A contrasting approach, voiced recently, is that the struggle to perform a nearly impossible piece is a crucial aspect of the work itself, even more important than its accurate representation. Whatever the merits of this latter approach, I doubt that it would have much appeal for Carter.

It is now several months later, and I have had a great deal more time to look at this vast and varied song-cycle, and I have been able to do so without a brass section in the background. "Anaphora," it turns out, illustrates two kinds of text setting that are prevalent in the *Mirror*. The first type I would describe as conveying an overall mood without endeavoring to illustrate every line or every word. Anaphora's first section, with its continuous bustling energy, provides a good example of this. The poet conjures up factory whistles, birds, bells, brilliant walls, and the energy of a day's beginning, but there is no one-to-one correspondence between specific words and musical images. Further, there is no literal musical translation of the poetic images—Messiaen's bird calls are not in evidence, there are no whistles blown from the percussion section, and no tolling chimes. Rather, all is suggested in a hazy impressionistic way by the frenzied instrumental lines, tremolos, and wide vocal leaps that wrap around the steady chordal structures. The vocal line participates in the fixed-pitch registration, lingering on the most important notes, or using them as turning points in the direction of the line. With its slower pacing, the voice part seems to fling itself over the entire stretch of the section to create an all-encompassing super-phrase.

The other type of text setting endeavors to more literally "paint" the text, and instances of this occur in the slower, more ruminative second part of "Anaphora." This is perhaps the most enjoyable kind of text-setting for composers to attempt because the poem itself often leads one down unexpected paths, and the collaborative aspect of the enterprise is raised to the foreground. The protagonist of the poem enters at (M. 22), and Carter chooses to change the mood of the song here rather than wait until the end of the first verse, thereby elevating the importance of the poem's narrative over its inner structure. The protagonist is "some ineffable creature;" literary critic Anne Stevenson suggests someone larger than life," the god Helios? Apollo? Christ? Someone we have missed, and always miss." In the poem, he "falls victim of long intrigue," "assumes mortal fatigue," and eventually is worn down by the events of the day. He is finally reduced to the "beggar in the park," yet at the poem's conclusion is still planning for future days and dreaming future dreams. The music from here on closely tracks and accentuates specific images. When our "ineffable creature" takes his earthly nature and dips into the day, the alto flute invokes the busy idioms of the "day music" preceding (M. 22). As he is "more slowly falling into sight," the forward motion is reined in, and a beautiful *sul ponticello* tremolo line emerges in the viola part, then recedes effortlessly. On the words, "darkening, condensing all his light," all reference to the opening bustle disappears. "Condensing" is set to a three-note chord F, F sharp and C, then added to that is the dyad D/G; these latter notes are an 11th apart, enveloping the held, closed-position trichord. These pitches bring back the sense of the very opening beat of the movement, without the hyper-activity. The two fifths, F/C and D/G, are made more poignant by the F sharp dissonance of the contrabass and an additional note, G sharp, in the vocal line. On the word "light," many of these pitches are held over as another important fifth, A/E, is struck between the oboe and the voice. These are the very first notes that the voice sings, and they are particularly expressive here. The oboe's E then descends to E flat in the viola, again as if mirroring the opening vocal line; the total effect of the moment seems to beautifully "condense" all the bustle of the day, distilling its primary ingredients. As the protagonist "sinks through the drift of bodies,…through the drift of classes," there are three sinking gestures, the piercing G flat-F (M. 43), followed by A-G sharp, and echoed by the oboe with E down to G sharp (M. 46). Following this passage, the voice, integrated as always, sinks, for the first time, to the two low twin roots: D and B.

As the poem ends, some of the energy of the beginning returns, as do the opening structures in their more urgent form, and I begin to suspect a reason for this setting's "minimalist," repetitive bent. The poem is about each day, every day. Every day "our creature" is consumed with the bustle of the day, every day starts out with so much promise and then all the tribulations of the world intrude. So the insistency seems warranted.

In ways both subtle and direct, Carter buoys all of the cycle's poems with astonishing resonance and a great range of emotion. The stark contrasts lift us from the intimacy of "Insomnia," to the boisterousness of the "View of the Capitol from the Library of Congress," to the touching evocation of the indefatigable bird of "Sandpiper." Carter's strong and sturdy musical voice has so many facets, yet always maintains an assured elegance and projects an uncanny sense of balance and proportion. I believe this music will always enjoy a place at the very pinnacle of American composition, and am honored to join in a 100th birthday salute to this most eloquent modern master.

ELLIOTT CARTER

* * * * *

Biography

A composer of over 60 orchestral, vocal and chamber works, LOUIS KARCHIN has been honored with performances of his music by such groups as the Chamber Music Society of Lincoln Center, the Louisville Orchestra, the Group for Contemporary Music, the Delta Ensemble of Amsterdam (Holland), and Spectrum Sonori (South Korea). In the spring of 2007, the Guggenheim Museum presented the world premiere of Karchin's 70-minute chamber opera, *Romulus*, and the following summer saw the premiere of his *Chesapeake Festival Overture* by the Orchestra di Stato della Romania at the Alba Music Festival (Italy), and by the Chesapeake Orchestra of the River Concert Series of St. Mary's College, Maryland. Karchin's music is recorded on New World, Albany and CRI labels, and 31 of his compositions are published by C. F. Peters Corporation. He is the recipient of numerous prizes and honors, including Koussevitzky and Barlow Foundation Commissions, and two awards each from the American Academy of Arts and Letters, the National Endowment for the Arts, and the Fromm Music Foundation at Harvard University. Mr. Karchin is Professor of Music at New York University, a conductor of the Chamber Players of the League-ISCM, and Co-director of the Washington Square Contemporary Music Society. He is also the author of essays on the music of composer Charles Wuorinen.

Charles Rosen (left) and Elliott Carter
Fred R. Conrad/ *The New York Times*/Redux

Elliott Carter: The Sustained Line

Charles Rosen

One aspect of Elliott Carter's music has not, I think, received the attention it deserves, as it sets him off from every other composer of his time: that is, the creation of expressive arabesque lines that reach eloquently from bass to treble, covering almost the entire musical space with an irregular and seemingly improvisatory continuity of developing metrical structure. This is found most often and best in the piano music, as it typically needs a unified tone color from the lowest bass to the highest treble to achieve its full effect. The earliest example is on the first page of the Piano Sonata with the *scorrevole* that follows the first slow openings bars:

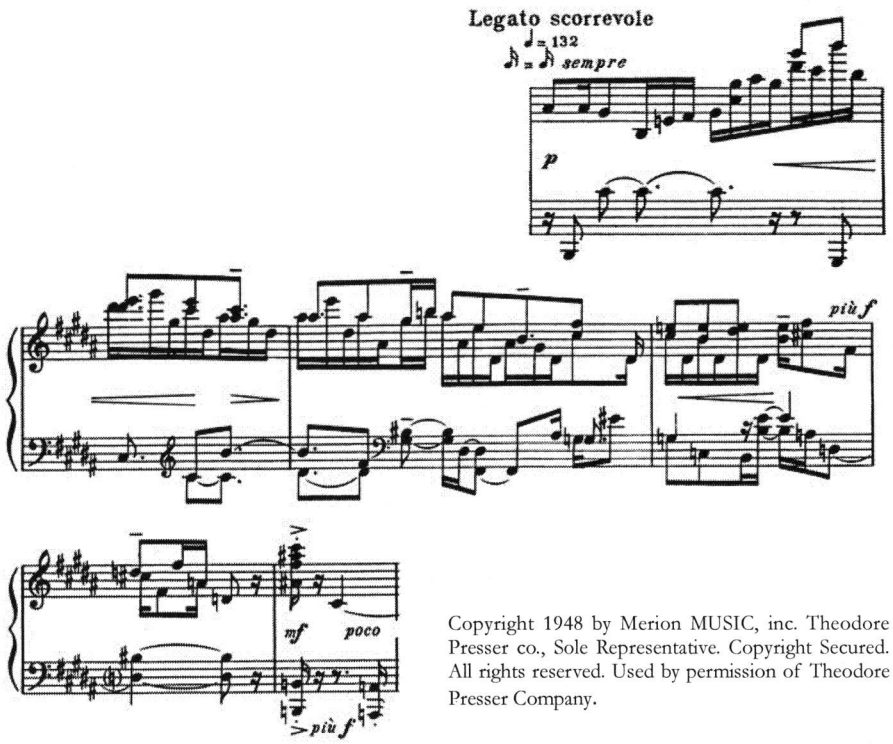

Copyright 1948 by Merion MUSIC, inc. Theodore Presser co., Sole Representative. Copyright Secured. All rights reserved. Used by permission of Theodore Presser Company.

Example 1

This freely presents the sonata's essential material of the series of overtones of the fifth starting from the B in the bass (F♯, C♯, G♯, D♯, A♯), and does so with a sweeping and expressive line. It has the expressive outline, within a context of tonality, of a major seventh at the opening resolving properly to a sixth—although the harmonic system of this sonata is not exactly orthodox triadic tonality, as the basic resolution of the work is a convincing ambiguity of either A-sharp or B-natural, an aspect announced on this opening page.

The next large-scale work for piano, the much later *Night Fantasies*, also has an expressive line similarly at the start of the first fast section following a brief slow opening page:

Night Fantasies by Elliott Carter. Copyright 1982 by Associated Music Publishers, Inc. (BMI) International Copyright Secured. All Rights Reserved. Used by Permission.

Example 2.

Here, however, the expressive line is limited to the higher register, but the different textures of the voices of the lower register are beautifully integrated with it and contribute to the expressive tension. More revealing of the power of the technique are bars 77 to 79, where the melodic line goes from the lowest B-flat on the piano to the highest C sharp, beginning slowly and gradually accelerating, with a built-in rubato effect of ritenuto at the più espressivo followed by a climactic acceleration at the end. What is traditional in this style of writing is that Carter has apparently revived here the old distinction between Haupstimme and Nebenstimme repudiated by most of the avant-garde like Boulez, Berio *et al* (although the repudiation in their case has been at best more in theory than in consistent practice, but what fragments of the old technique are left in their work is never exploited as whole-heartedly as in Carter), and, indeed, the Nebenstimmen in this passage of Carter are by no means completely subordinate. Nevertheless, the construction is as much dependent on expressive vocal style as it is in Mozart or Chopin although exceeding the vocal compass of any singer (as it so often does in Chopin as well).

Night Fantasies by Elliott Carter. Copyright 1982 by Associated Music Publishers, Inc. (BMI) International Copyright Secured. All Rights Reserved. Used by Permission.

Example 3.

In Carter's most recent work, the technique plays an even more prominent role. It dominates the middle section of *90+*, for example, which merits a brief examination of at least a few bars to see how Carter is able to achieve a special kind of expressive effect normally possible within tonality without resorting to the reactionary revival of tonal elements that most other composers need to incorporate (the profoundly expressive character of Milton Babbitt's *Widow's Lament in Springtime*, for example, depends on the fact that the row outlines a major triad in one version, and therefore a minor triad in the inversion, and the expressive character of Schoenberg's minuet from opus 25 derives from a mimicry by phrasing of the effect of the tonal resolution of a dissonant appoggiatura into a consonant harmony).

In *90+*, the expressive arabesque line is a long two pages and opens:

90+ Copyright 1994 by Hendon Music, Inc. A Boosey & Hawkes Company. Copyrighted for all countries. All rights reserved. Reprinted by permission.

Example 4.

This is marked *molto espressivo*, the kind of direction that has provoked the disapproval of intransigent modernist critics who feel that Carter should have restricted himself to a more austere version of modernism, and find such a return to eloquence compromising. The structure of the grand legato upper voice does not employ tonal harmony, although it has the expressive intensity associated with tonality. This arises from Carter's use of the acoustic property of intervals, a use that we might call pre-tonal because they contributed to the development of tonality (that is, certain intervals like the fifth and the tenth have a more consonant or stable quality as they are related by the overtones of the lower note). Carter's practice is dependent, I believe, on his understanding of the horizontal element of traditional voice-leading, where the harmony is implied by the successive elements of the melodic outline: in the passage quoted, the opening twelve notes of the soprano line emphasize the two major sevenths (D to C sharp and C-sharp to C-natural), nuanced by the intermediate notes and by the staccato bass part, which gives the opening a jagged intensity that is relieved by the outline of the sixths that follow (C to E, and E to A-flat, the latter tempered by the F that comes after and makes a seventh with the E, but re-emphasizes the interval of the sixth through the A natural that succeeds). This creates a pattern of tension and release that is strictly non-tonal but exceedingly effective.

The same principles are at work even more strikingly in the magnificent opening phrase of the soloist that follows the short slow introductory English horn solo in the *Dialogues* for piano and orchestra:

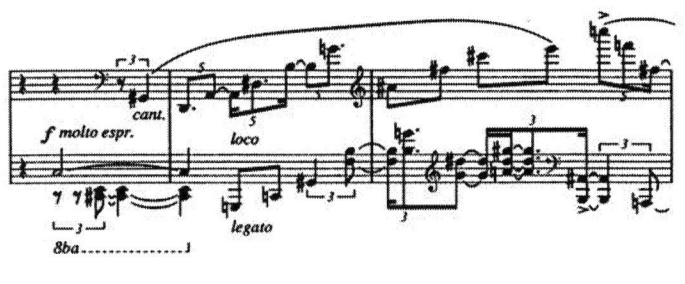

Dialogues, Copyright 2003 by Hendon Music, Inc. A Boosey & Hawkes Company. Copyrighted for all countries. All rights reserved. Reprinted by permission.

Example 5.

Here the intervals set in relief begin with tritons (D to G-sharp, A to D-sharp), follow with sixths (B to G, A-sharp to F-sharp), and continue to accelerate with the falling fifths (C to F, F-sharp to B, D-sharp to G-sharp), and end with emphatic minor sevenths in both left and right hands. Once again the direction is, very reasonably, *molto espressivo.* I have chosen only one aspect of the harmonic character of this passage and there is of course much more to say. Nevertheless, in most of his works (the string quartets and the piano concerto are among the best examples), Carter has been exceptionally sensitive to the specific acoustic character of the different intervals, exploiting concentrations of them to give a different acoustic atmosphere and affective personality to the individual passages and sections with a technique that is not essentially very different from the one that Bartok used in the *Scherzo per le coppie* in the Concerto for Orchestra, although Carter's is less dogmatic and relentless. In the examples we have seen, it enables Carter to create the changes of tension essential to an expressive line. Carter's response to the acoustic character of musical material is not so much theoretical as intuitive, and it explains the affective variety and complexity of his work.

* * * * *

Biography

The breadth of **Charles Rosen's** endeavors reflects a remarkable synthesis of performing musician, scholar, writer and lecturer. First, however, he remains one of the most widely respected pianists of our time, internationally acclaimed for his performances and recordings of works ranging from Bach to those by the 20th-century's most important composers. Mr. Rosen's unique combination of musical sensitivity and powerful intelligence produces interpretations of exceptional understanding and impact. He has been heard in major concert halls and at leading festivals throughout the world and continues to perform in music capitals here and abroad.

Mr. Rosen is particularly renowned for his interpretations of Beethoven and the Romantic repertoire, inheriting the great Romantic piano tradition in a direct line from some of its most illustrious proponents. Born in New York City, Mr. Rosen was enrolled at The Juilliard School at the age of six, leaving five years later to study with Moriz Rosenthal, a pupil of Liszt, and his wife, Hedwig Kanner, a pupil of Theodor Leschetizky. In 1951, the same year that Mr. Rosen made his New York debut, he received his doctorate in French literature from Princeton University and made his first recording: the world premiere recording of

Souvenirs

Frederic Rzewski

Memories, like the events that produce them, do not come when summoned. They arrive chaotically. They may lie hidden until, suddenly, they appear at their pleasure; or not. Composers writing about other composers inevitably end up talking about themselves, and I can't avoid it either. My memories of Elliott Carter are closely bound to milestones of my life.

Once in the seventies we visited the Carters in Waccabuc. The kids went skating on the frozen pond. They pulled Elliott along behind them, like two ponies towing a sled. Much to their amusement, he pretended to be afraid, crying "Oh! I'm falling!" although he was clearly in perfect form, having since childhood skated on frozen ponds.

Elliott and Helen were a very important part of our lives since the early sixties. He was a model not only for me, but also for my wife Nicole, who loved his music, his wisdom and experience, culture and personality. This exemplary model of creative discipline, reaching me as it did from two different directions, exerted a great force on me, and helped me to get through some difficult times. Nicole writes (2007):

Quand je pense à Elliott, je pense beaucoup à sa bibliothèque que j'ai beaucoup fouillée quand il était en voyage et que je restais là, à New York. Ce qui me frappait, c'était que ces choix de livres correspondaient à mes choix, en Europe, aux choix de nous Européens assez internationaux. Auteurs italiens non traduits, russes dans de bonnes traductions, français en français (Elliott m'a raconté que le français avait pratiquement été sa première langue, et qu'ensuite, à l'école à New York, il avait du s'efforcer de ne pas toujours corriger son professeur de français), allemands, tout melé, Moravia, Brecht, Baudelaire, Camus. Yourcenar.... on en discutait puis quand il revenait. Conversations simples, sincères, approfondies, belles. Quand il venait avec Helen à Rome, à la villa Aurelia, les musiciens italiens venaient le chercher, ce qui visiblement lui faisait grand plaisir, Souvent on dinait frugalement dans l'austère Académie Américaine, on parlait dans ses vastes salons confortables à coté du billard ou jouaient les plus jeunes avec cette rumeur caractéristique.

Elliott Carter and Frederic Rzewski, Berlin 1963
Courtesy of Nicole Rzewski

SOUVENIRS

When I think of Elliott, I think of his library, which I often examined when he was traveling and I stayed there in New York. I was struck by his choice of books, which corresponded to my choices in Europe, to the international choices of us Europeans. Italian authors in the original language, Russian writers in good translations, French writers in French (Elliott told me that his first language was actually French; later in a New York school, he had to restrain himself from constantly correcting his French teacher), Germans, everything mixed together: Moravia, Brecht, Baudelaire, Camus, Yourcenar, and so on. We talked about it later, when he returned. Simple conversations, sincere, in depth, beautiful. When he came to Rome with Helen, in the Villa Aurelia, the Italian musicians came to visit, which clearly gave him great pleasure. Often we had a frugal meal in the austere American Academy; we talked in the vast, comfortable rooms, next to the billiards where the younger people were playing, with their characteristic sounds.)

Helen was like a mother to Nicole and grandmother to our children. Packages would arrive regularly with clothes and other gifts. Helen paid for our daughter Noemi's orthodontic treatment. Our children remember her with fondness. Noemi recalls that Helen told her to drink lots of milk. When she came to visit, her pants were too long so Helen made her roll them up and pull up her socks. Helen's salads were so delicious that she acquired a love for salad that continues to this day. In remembering Elliott's studio, Noemi writes (2007):

> ...*sempre pieno di carte e sul muro, di fronte alla scrivania, un cartello con una scritta in italiano: "un posto per ogni cosa, ogni cosa al suo posto"; le pareti rosse della casa, e i quadri di pittori famosi (un disegno di Picasso, e un quadro di Mirò); una scultura di Helen. una testa di donna di pietra nera (o bronzo?) abbastanza stilizzata, allungata, fine, con gli occhi come nelle figure di Modigliani. Mi ricordo che a Elliott gli piace molto Calvino...*

(...always full of papers, and on the wall in front of his desk, a placard in Italian: "a place for everything, everything in its place"; the red walls of the house, and the pictures by famous artists (a drawing by Picasso, a picture by Mirò); one of Helen's sculptures, a woman's head in black stone (or bronze?), rather stylized, stretched out, with eyes like those of Modigliani figures. I remember that Elliott liked Calvino a lot...)

I suppose that made Helen in some way my mother-in-law, although I never thought of her that way. For me she was a friend, whose humor I loved, and who often gave good advice. I think she was probably the best-dressed woman I have ever met. Her taste in clothes was exquisitely reserved and elegant.

She was hard on me sometimes, but she was usually right. "Always aim high," she said, "and remember, there's nothing sadder than an old hippie."

I have always admired his physical stamina, as I admire his intelligence, wit, and broad knowledge of culture. I watched him in Waccabuc chopping wood, like a Yankee farmer. We chatted about music, literature, and politics. We discussed the question whether democracy was an aging form. Should there be a fourth branch of government, representing finance and industry? He found some merit in such thoughts, but didn't think it was a good idea to change the constitution.

At the Pontino Festival south of Rome, we listened to a lengthy discourse by an Italian architect about architecture as the only truly avant-garde form. We laughed over the notion that architecture was, after all, merely a matter of putting one stone on top of another, and could hardly be expected to produce anything new.

I first met Elliott in the Spring of 1960, when I played in a concert at the Third Street Music School Settlement. I admired his music, which I had only heard in recordings, as it were from afar. We met again in Rome in the early sixties. By that time I was married, with one child, Alexis, and another, Ico, on the way. I think it was largely because of Helen that we all went to Berlin in the fall of 1963 with a scholarship from the Ford Foundation. Helen thought that Rome was not a good place for small children, and that the air in Berlin would be good for them. There I met two of Elliott's students, Alvin Curran and Joel Chadabe, both of whom became lifelong friends. I also met other people who have been important for me, like Louis Andriessen, Vinko Globokar, and Yuji Takahashi. (It was Yuji's son, Yujiko, who gave Ico his name: Iko). I myself was never his student. I once brought him a score, hoping to get some tips on orchestration. "Oh no," he said, "you know much more about orchestration than I do!"

But of course I learned a lot simply by being around him and Helen, talking about this and that, anything from Charles Ives to disposable diapers. That time in Berlin cemented a relationship that has never gone away, largely because of the very close relationship that developed between our wives.

The next time we came into longer contact was in the seventies, in New York City, where I lived for five years with my family (by that time we had a third son, Jan, born in 1970). It was a difficult time, in 1973 neither of us had a steady job or any hope of getting one; the Carters helped us pay the rent. Finally I got a part-time job teaching for two days every two weeks at the Art Institute of Chicago. I wanted to tell the art students about new American music so I chose three pieces as a point of departure: Carter's Concerto for Orchestra, Cage's *HPSCHD*, and Ornette Coleman's *Skies Of America*. Unlike each other as these things might seem, to me they were all quintessentially American. I think Elliott didn't particularly care for this idea.

The Carters were friends with the Stravinskys, and visited them periodically. Elliott described to me after one such meeting how Stravinsky beckoned him to his studio, to show him "how" he wrote music: He laid out scraps of paper on the floor, of different shapes and sizes, with music written on them, and shuffled them around to make various interesting configurations.

Although we don't see eye to eye on everything, there is very little we can't talk about. Perhaps it has to do with a humanist view of culture, and a certain New England tradition of tolerance. Whether the subject is Proust, Velazquez, or Cicero, Elliott often makes some brilliant connection that puts the question in a new light. Or he will close the debate with some witty remark, indicating that it's time to change the subject.

In June of 2006, Ursula Oppens and I had dinner with Elliott at their club in New York. Somehow the conversation turned to the Austro-Hungarian Empire, which Elliott denounced as decadent. I objected, pointing out that it had produced great writers, poets, painters, and composers, and that, in this respect at least, it was better than the American empire. "That's not saying much!" was his rejoinder.

Coming out of the club, we waited while Ursula went off to hail a taxi. A water bug scuttled across the sidewalk. Elliott had some trouble walking, but with no trouble at all lashed out several times with one foot in a karate-like maneuver. (The insect, itself an educated New Yorker, escaped.)

I visited him in August 2007, at one point in the conversation he interjected, "you don't have a publisher, do you?" I said, no, I thought publishers were no longer useful: parasites at best, in fact, "oh, worse than that!" he said, laughing.

In Berlin he complained about composers like Earle Brown and Bruno Maderna, who were experimenting with semi-improvised orchestral pieces, like Brown's *Available Forms*. They were competing unfairly with composers like himself, who worked for months to prepare a score, by offering cut-rate music on the marketplace.

His tastes have always been broad. He likes both Stockhausen and Puccini. At the same time, his judgments on music tend to be swift, leaving little room for appeal. I once played a recording for him of some of Giovanna Marini's work, which I found interesting for its blend of traditional Sardinian and Sicilian vocal techniques with classical and avant-garde forms. Elliott categorically rejected this music, saying that it contained nothing original. (I had to admit that, from a modernist perspective, he was right.)

Elliott was invited to the White House, to be presented with a prize by Ronald Reagan. I saw a photograph in which he was shaking hands with the President. We met shortly afterwards. I asked him how he could do it. Why didn't he just refuse, like the poet Robert Lowell, who was offered a similar honor during the Vietnam War?

"Not at all," he said, "Reagan was kind and entertaining." He sat at the same table with the President at lunch. A woman asked Reagan if his job wasn't too stressful, "no, not at all, it is very satisfying" came the answer. He then, according to Carter, told a story of two psychoanalysts, one old, the other young, who often meet in the elevator at the end of the day. The younger of the two, worn out, sweating, observes that his older colleague is always calm. Finally, he asks the older man how he can be so relaxed after listening to all those terrible stories, "Who listens?" he responds.

Elliott is a living example of the life-giving power of music. His absolute dedication to his art has been a constant source of inspiration for me. In many critical moments of my life, merely thinking of him has given me the courage to go on.

(October, 2007)

Elliott Carter (right) with Ursala Oppens and Frederic Rzewski

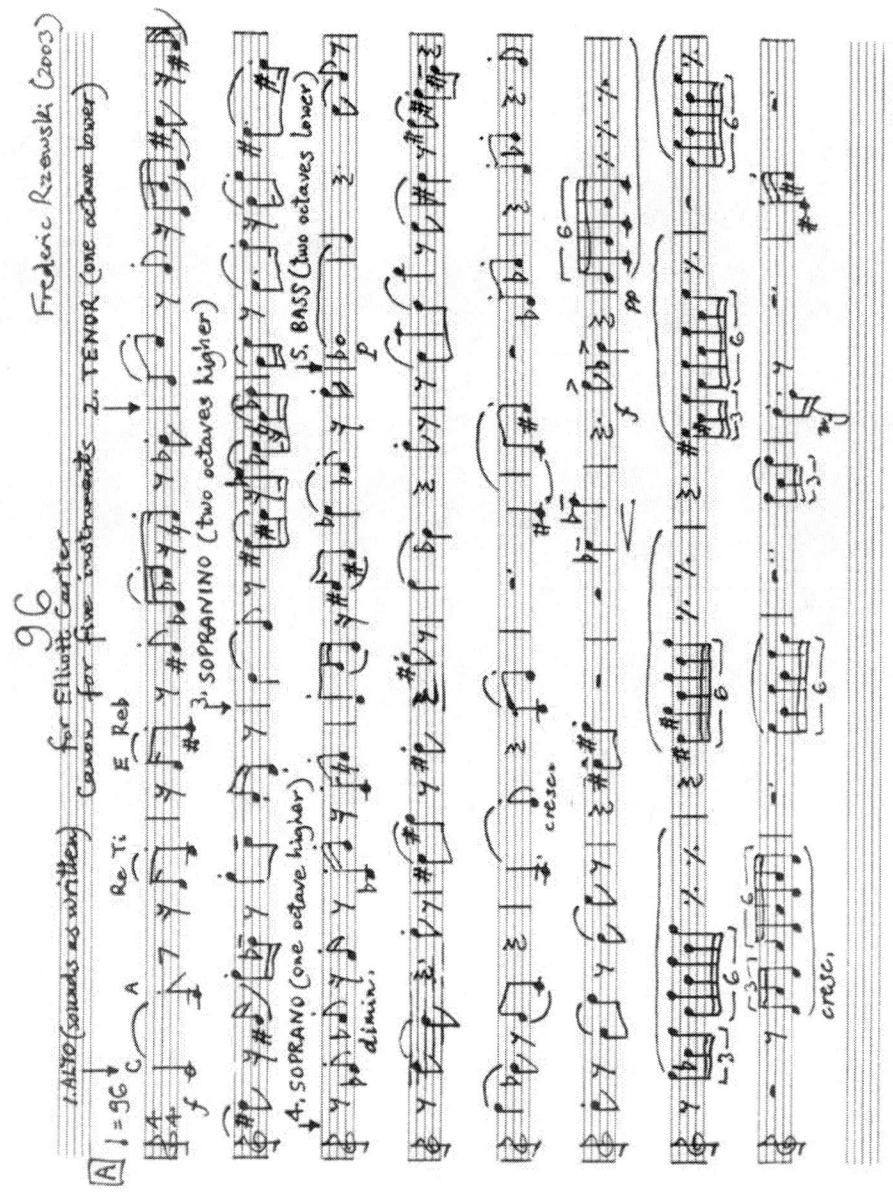

SOUVENIRS

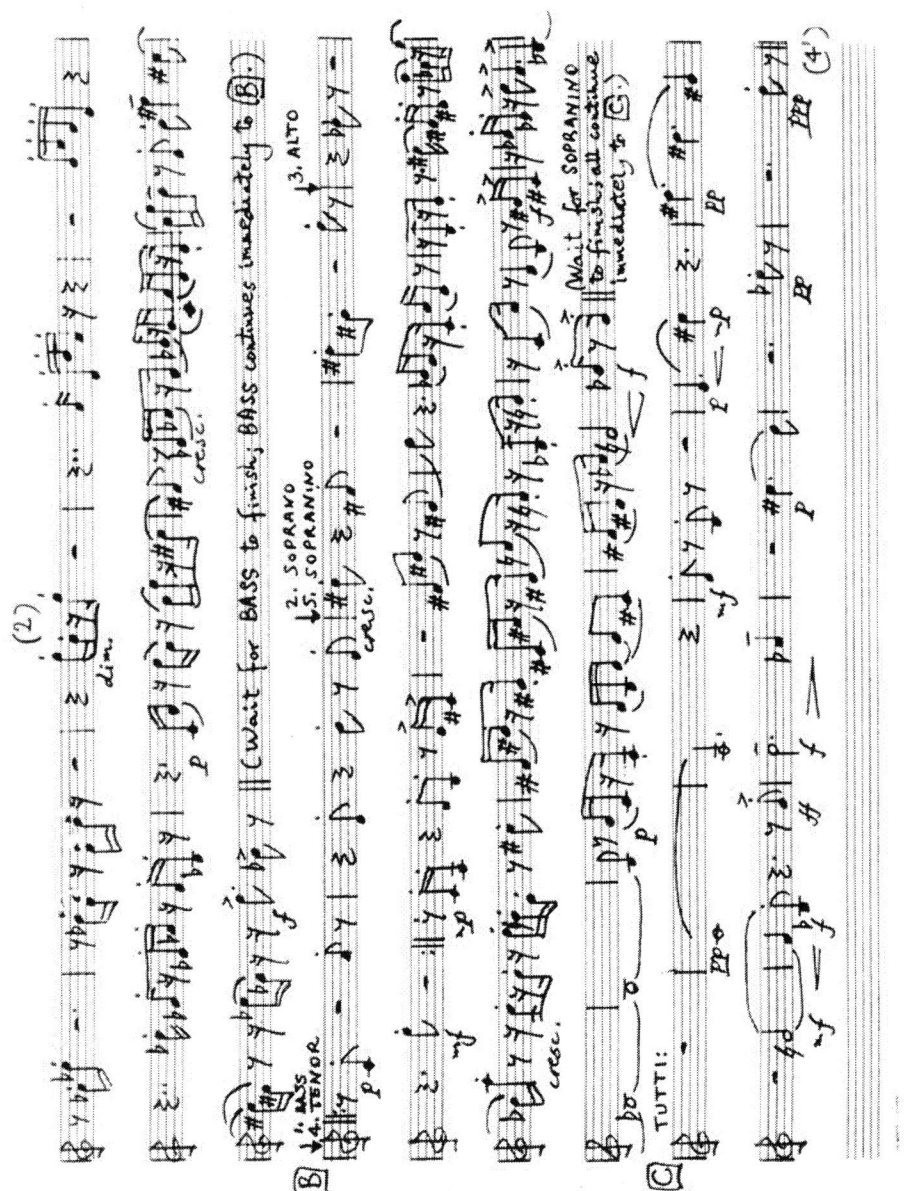

73

* * * * *

Biography

Born in Westfield, Massachusetts in 1938, **Frederic Rzewski** studied music at first with Charles Mackey of Springfield, and subsequently with Walter Piston, Roger Sessions, and Milton Babbitt at Harvard and Princeton universities. He went to Italy in 1960, where he studied with Luigi Dallapiccola and met Severino Gazzelloni, with whom he performed in a number of concerts, thus beginning a career as a performer of new piano music. In Rome in the mid-sixties, together with Alvin Curran and Richard Teitelbaum, he formed the MEV (Musica Elettronica Viva) group, which quickly became known for its pioneering work in live electronics and improvisation. Rzewski has recorded *The People United; North American Ballads*, and *Squares*; and the *Sonata* and *De Profundis* on hat ART records (CD 6066, 6089, & 6134); *Four Pieces* on Vanguard; and *Bumps, Andante con Moto,* and *The Turtle and the Crane* for Newport Classic. "Rzewski Plays Rzewski", a box of seven discs of piano music performed by the composer, was released by Nonesuch in September, 2002. From 1983 to 2003 Rzewski was Professor of Composition at the Conservatoire Royal de Musique in Liège, Belgium. He has also taught at the Yale School of Music, the University of Cincinnati, the State University of New York at Buffalo, the California Institute of the Arts, the University of California at San Diego, Mills College, the Royal Conservatory of the Hague, the Hochschule der Künste in Berlin, and the Hochschule für Musik in Karlsruhe.

Beginnings and Endings—
Plus a Conversation

Richard Wilson

My acquaintance with Elliott Carter the person, began on December 20, 1969 when he served as moderator for the Composers' Forum held at the Donnell Library Auditorium in New York City. I was one of two composers featured on that occasion, the other being Joel Chadabe, who had studied with Carter. My then very limited acquaintance with Elliott Carter the composer, had begun in 1964 as his Second String Quartet was performed in Rome when I was living at the American Academy. That work thrilled me and led me to investigate the much longer First Quartet, the score and recording of which were in the Academy library. Back in New York, like many young composers who attended the series of his frequent premieres in the next years (*Concerto for Orchestra*, Third String Quartet, *Symphony for Three Orchestra* etc.), I began to view him as the most innovative and exciting figure in American music. But I was in awe both of the man and his music. It was not until the Huddersfield Festival in 1983 that I got to know him and his formidable wife Helen well enough to feel comfortable in their presence. His music continued to induce in me a certain sense of inadequacy.

It was the premiere of the *Duo for Violin and Piano* that particularly challenged and even discouraged me. The work was done twice, before and after intermission. The second performance was not recognizable to me as something I had just heard. The apparent complexity of the work put it beyond my comprehension. I have since heard Rolf Schulte and Ursula Oppens give riveting performances of this same work, and I have not felt defeated by it. But that was later.

Very soon after this experience, I attended a full evening of Carter's music in London conducted by Oliver Knussen. Hearing the *Double Concerto* live for the first time gave me the feeling of being on a sonic adventure into a strange and intriguing environment—a sensation that is vivid in my memory today. The keenness of his aural imagination in dealing with so many unpitched percussion sounds staggered me. Every detail seemed precisely in place. Any loss of faith in this composer, occasioned by the *Duo*, was quickly restored.

From the start, one particular aspect of Carter's music impressed me. Whereas the eighteenth-century symphony might typically begin with a call to attention and stating of the main key; and would predictably end with an emphatic tonal cadence in that key, Elliott Carter's works tended to show an unusually imaginative approach to both extremes. There is no predicting how they will begin; and how they end is only marginally less surprising.

Certain of Carter's earlier works have 'logical' endings. The Cello Sonata begins with the piano as clock and cello as rhapsodist. It ends with the cello ticking away pizzicato and the piano providing connected notes of irregular length—an unmistakable reversal of roles. (Of course one should not neglect the witty surprise of the triple octave harmonic combined with the plucked C-string that is actually the last sound heard.) The First String Quartet, in a detail famously inspired by film (Cocteaus's *Le Sang d'un Poete*), ends with a continuation of the first violin's opening line—which was heard more than forty minutes earlier.

With the *Double Concerto* as model, an unusual number of later works end with an emphatic, typically very loud, climax after which the music reverberates and undergoes sonic decay. In the case of the single instrument concertos, this post-climactic passage—an *exodos*, to use a term from Greek drama which might have appeal to Carter—gives a valedictory opportunity to the solo instrument and whatever 'concertino' may have been associated with it.

The coda of the *Double Concerto* begins with a crash and reverberates for seventy-one bars during which four strands of music fluctuate in conflicting wave patterns. Because of the length of this section, about two and one-half minutes, as well as the complexity of the texture, it may prove difficult for the uninitiated listener to grasp fully the overall design, which is one of carefully controlled sonic decay from the dynamic climax that finally stops on an amusing click in the claves. The triple forte blast in bar 619 risks being forgotten in the energetic and consuming dialogue between the piano and harpsichord and their associated ensembles. Later works will show much greater clarity in the presentation of the dynamic highpoint and its contrasting aftermath.

This is evident already in the Piano Concerto, finished four years later. This work begins and ends with the piano alone quietly occupying itself with three-note sonorities. The orchestra reaches a stabbing climax, marked **sfff**, at bar 663. The next fifteen bars are largely reverberation and decay with final appearances of the group of instruments associated with the solo piano: flute, English horn, bass clarinet and solo strings mostly playing *pianissimo*. Unlike the opening, where the piano's pitches gradually reach upward, here the notes push downward, ending on the lowest G-sharp.

In the Oboe Concerto, written twenty-two years later, we find the orchestral climax, which features triple-*forte* karate-chops, in bar 403. The remaining thirty bars are an oboe-dominated *tranquillo* which culminates with the oboe delineating its musical space, which is rather more rigidly limited than that of the violin, cello, or clarinet. High A is directly followed by low B-flat; the final pitch is C-sharp, which falls just shy of the midpoint of this space. High A is the first note played by the oboe in this work, and low B-flat receives an almost obsessive amount of emphasis as a *fortissimo* pedal point in the passage bars 186-197: seven loud, low B-flats.

The Violin Concerto of 1990 concludes with an especially quick aftermath. The orchestra reaches a climactic, triple-*forte tutti* chord in bar 620; the work ends five bars later, the solo violin descending alone from a stratospheric B (so high it is almost off the piano keyboard) with music marked 'very dramatically' and '*marcatissimo*' and punctuated by chords with up to six notes. At the very ending, muted strings join in a quick, gossamer cadence, *pianissimo* with the solo on a high E-flat.

The Clarinet Concerto of 1996 is one of the relatively few Carter works that actually ends loud. As with the Third String Quartet, there is no echoing coda. The hyperactive solo clarinet finishes the work on an emphatic tuning A. (Example 1, p. 83)

The Cello Concerto of 2001 on the other hand returns to the more familiar design. We find loud orchestral *tuttis*—a series of screaming sonorities, with full-orchestra attacks against a sheet of sustained string sound. After this, the cello carries on for nearly a minute with virtuosic agility until it resorts to pizzicato, guitar style. The very last gesture is a pair of plucked harmonics in an optimistic, rising perfect fourth.

Between the concertos for clarinet and cello, Carter composed the *Asko Concerto* for a chamber ensemble of sixteen players. The overall design involves two trios, two duos, a quintet and a solo. The solo is for bassoon, and it is a two-minute extravaganza that is followed by a set of accelerating staccato chords from the full ensemble—another loud ending. (Example 2, pp. 84-5)

The *Boston Concerto* of 2002, inspired by William Carlos Williams's poem "Rain," contains passages clearly meant to suggest precipitation.

Its ending is approached with a *descrescendo* of repeated notes, many of them pizzicatos, in conflicting rhythmic patterns. Although there are some loud staccato chords there is no real sense of an orchestral climax. The last note is a plucked B below middle C—B presumably for Boston. (Example 3, p. 86)

The texture of pizzicatos found in the *Boston Concerto* may have its antecedent in String Quartet No. 5, composed in 1995, which ends with a considerable section of plucking in cross rhythms—a corn popping effect—before the last eight seconds, where *arco* playing returns for a brief comment from each of the four players.

In *Dialogues for Piano and Orchestra*, composed in 2003, we again find an emphatic climactic cadence in the orchestra. This has the effect of freezing time: the piano provides single notes covering the keyboard from top to bottom against a quietly sustained background. The piano shares its line with the clarinet; a scattering of trombone notes seem left over from the *tutti*.

The only generality that occurs about how Carter's works begin is that, where an impression of chaos or disorder prevails at the very start, a specific instrumental character will tend to appear and establish a focus. A particularly vivid example of this is not a solo concerto, but rather the *Symphony of Three Orchestras*. We hear first quiet, ethereal strings in the high register. The sonority is momentarily consonant, then becomes a cluster. Rapid piano repeated notes high up usher in piccolo twittering, other winds join, and the trumpet sneaks in on a high A-flat. This single note broadens into a trill, then spirals out into a chromatic line. This captivating trumpet solo goes on for more than a minute, gently speeding and slowing. Whether or not we know that the intention is to portray the wheeling of a sea gull, an image made vivid in Frank Scheffer's film, (*A Labyrinth of Time*) we are in no doubt that the work is purposefully underway. (Example 4, p. 87)

In the earlier *Concerto for Orchestra*, the listener is drawn in by quiet, unpitched percussion: a drum roll without snares, gong, then snares, then more gong and cymbals. Dynamic action precedes the introduction of pitch, which comes as high A-flat in string harmonics. Pulsation in the harp, featuring repeated Gs; a dotted figure in the trumpet, an eloquent rising minor seventh in the tuba. A gradual crescendo underlies the swells and fades of the percussion: we perceive two levels of dynamic activity going at once. A violent buildup introduces a staccato clock motif in the trumpets and other brass; the ticking is punctuated by karate-chops. The piano, joined by mallet instruments, establishes order and focus. Familiarity with the *Double Concerto* and the Piano Concerto, the immediately preceding major works, gives this opening a sense of connection to a much larger project, as though Carter had in mind his entire oeuvre in which one piece leads directly to the next with little interruption in continuity.

How solo instrument concertos begin necessarily involves the placement of the first appearance of the soloist. The Oboe Concerto opens with a low, murky, menacing sonority comprised of contrabasses, cellos, bass clarinet, and timpani. As has been mentioned, the oboe so to speak falls from the sky. Its squealing high A is so high a note that one hardly recognizes the distinctive color of the oboe—it might as well be an E-flat clarinet. As it descends into a more normal register, it plays a multiphonic—two pitches at once in a distorted timbre, that further confuses the ear. The character of its music is lyrical, and the instrument seems to be exploring its available musical space. The lower limit, the B-flat mentioned above, is sounded before the orchestra takes over in a burst of assertiveness.

The Clarinet Concerto opens loudly, *in medias res*, with the solo clarinet entering directly after an orchestral "call to attention." The soloist's rapid, athletic figuration gives way briefly to the piano.

The Violin Concerto similarly opens up a Pandora's Box of activity: scrubbing strings, swirling winds, hammer strokes from trumpets and trombone. The violin exhibits a contrasting affect, more expressive, lyrical, and legato. It ruminates in its low register, apparently indifferent to the confusion surrounding it. Before the first minute is up, it acquires a more assertive, emphatic and dramatic persona.

Like the Piano Concerto, the Cello Concerto begins and ends with the solo instrument. Karate-chop chords, highly dissonant, interrupt the cello's opening rhetorical statements.

Similar loud chords open the *Asko Concerto* but as each is struck, a varying set of instruments remains sounding, so that the after-resonance produces successively different instrumental colors. A gradually accelerating central strand vies with short, rapid punctuations. (Example 5, p. 88)

The rain-inspired *Boston Concerto* begins with a burst that unleashes a scattering of pizzicatos combined with flute twittering, a measured trill in the harp, and finally a trumpet rising through a quintuplet to high A: this becomes the focus that convinces us the argument of the piece has truly begun. (Examples 6 and 7, pp. 90-91)

Most unusually, the *Dialogues for Piano and Orchestra* begin with an unaccompanied English horn solo. As the English horn was prominent as one of the instruments in the concertino of the Piano Concerto of 1964-5, one takes this to be an oblique reference to that earlier work. Here the piano enters with Carter's version of the upward flourish at the opening of the *Emperor Concerto*. (Examples 8 and 9, pp. 91, 92)

Describing in this way how works begin and conclude falls considerably short of explaining why the openings and endings seem so apt. Conversations with Elliott Carter have led me to believe that he plans his endings well before his draft has reached that point in the creative process. So he knows, as it were, where he is going as he composes. How he arrives at the beginnings is something one could hardly expect him to disclose, if he even has anything to say on the subject.

Of course, works with text or a dramatic situation offer up a suggestion about how to begin and end. Carter's one opera, *What Next?*, sports an overture made up entirely of unpitched percussion. This recalls the *Double Concerto* but is dramatically apt as the opera's plot begins with a car crash. The first noun of the libretto's text is 'star' and the individual singers begin with sibilants that emerge from scraping, sizzling sounds drawn largely from cymbals. (Example 10, p. 93) The opera ends with a staccato orchestral chord, **sfff**, immediately followed by one of opera's mainstay effects: a sustained high C sung by Rose, the operatic diva. (Example 11, p. 94)

What occurs between the opening and the ending of any Carter work cannot easily be generalized. If any one observation is useful it is that the music typically takes on a conversational character: individual instruments, or groups of instruments, are personified and exchange commentary—some gruff, some light-hearted, some passionate—with each other. Conversation is important to Elliott Carter, an unusually and surprisingly sociable man. My wife, Dee, and I have visited him many times, often for tea, during which conversation has been lively, surprising, and memorable. Just after one such visit, on October 3, 2005, we sat down and made notes on what we could remember of what was said. Without quoting directly from any of us, I have made a sketch giving some idea of the range of subjects covered in one cup of tea.

Presented with a program from the 2005 Bard Music Festival, Elliott wanted to know how Copland's music had fared. He seemed surprised to learn that his Wind Quintet had been included in the program. We discussed *Grohg, Symphonic Ode, Statements, Music for the Theater* and *The Tender Land*. Bard had presented Blitzstein's *Regina*. Elliott mentioned having seen this years ago and liked it. He had known Blitzstein from his Paris years.

Elliott asked what the Bard Festival was planning for the summer of 2006. When he learned it would be Liszt he mentioned the works he particularly liked: *Valle d'Obermann* and, surprisingly, *Les Preludes*. He had been reading the Alan Walker volumes about Liszt and was intrigued that he had studied orchestration fairly late in life.

We talked about Schumann's *Genoveva*, the music of which Elliott knew and liked although he couldn't make much of the plot. At the mention of Meyerbeer, he said he had heard *L'Africain* at the Met when young and liked it a lot.

When he was a student at Harvard there was a summer scholarship for study in Munich. He spent two summers there, hearing a lot of opera (Wagner and Strauss particularly) but did not learn enough German. He has been practicing German irregular verbs ever since. and likes to do this before falling asleep.

Elliott was reading Proust in French and enjoying the remarkable detail. He marvels at the structure of sentences that contain long parenthetical digressions with a mixture of genders that finally make you wonder what is going on. He recounted an episode about Marcel and his aunt, who is about to have her photograph taken and has gone and bought a new outfit—which displeases Marcel. He talked about the bit of music that Proust uses as a motif. I mentioned that Henze wrote the violin and piano music used in the film with Jeremy Irons. He has known Henze for many years. He recalled that he and Helen attended the premiere of *Elegy for Young Lovers* along with Wystan Auden (who wrote the libretto with Chester Kallman).

Elliott had seen that the new biography of Edmund Wilson was featured in *The Times Book Review*. Wilson had once tried to get Elliott taken on as music critic of *The New Yorker*. He said he was very glad this did not come to pass, thinking it would have been a big mistake. Edmund Wilson once called and invited him to go along to a lecture by Vladimir Nabokov. It turned out to be all in Russian and therefore incomprehensible.

Conversation then turned to the subject of travel, Elliott is planning a trip to Basel. Charles Rosen is at a festival in the south of Rome, where it is very hot. It is a place Helen and Elliott know and have visited, he commented that whenever they opened their car door, swarms of beggar children appeared.

The mention of Dresden and Prague evoked memories of his visits there with Helen. He seems able to recall exactly where they stayed, the location of the hotel, details about the lobbies, the rooms they had, who they met where, and what music he heard.

He is looking forward to Tanglewood and the performances of various of his works. He was up there with Virgil Blackwell getting some young harpists to try out certain effects he wanted for the piece he wrote for the Nash Ensemble. He complains about the difficulty of getting a harp part that satisfies harpists and doesn't cause them to re-write it.

Elliott has also finished a six-minute piano piece for Peter Serkin. He has just learned that Daniel Barenboim has decided to play the piano parts that begin and end the orchestral work written (also during this year) for Chicago Symphony to mark Barenboim's departure. The premiere is to be the same night that James Levine is doing his *Three Allusions* in Boston. He must make the difficult decision of which performance to attend. Many things are also coming up in Europe, Heinz Holliger will be doing his Oboe Quartet in several cities in Italy.

As a next project, Elliott is planning a setting of Wallace Stevens' poems for moderately high soprano (not above A-flat) and about twelve to fourteen instruments. This will be performed by James Levine and the Met Chamber Players. Elliott has read through all the Stevens' poems twice before making a selection.

He wonders whether at some point, given his age, he shouldn't simply draw a line and say, "that's all," after a pause he says, " but it is hard to stop.

Example 1: Clarinet Concerto by Elliott Carter, meas. 444-447

Clarinet Concerto, Copyright 1997 by Hendon Music, Inc. A Boosey & Hawkes Company. Copyrighted for all countries. All rights reserved. Reprinted by permission.

ELLIOTT CARTER

Example 2: Asko Concerto by Elliott Carter meas. 290-296

Asko Concerto, Copyright 2000 by Hendon Music, Inc. A Boosey & Hawkes Company. Copyrighted for all countries. All rights reserved. Reprinted by permission

Example 2., cont.

Example 3: Boston Concerto by Elliott Carter meas. 354-358

Boston Concerto, Copyright 2002 by Hendon Music, Inc. A Boosey & Hawkes Company. Copyrighted for all countries. All rights reserved. Reprinted by permission.

Example 4: Symphony of Three Orchestras by Elliott Carter meas. 1-5

Symphony of Three Orchestras by Elliott Carter Copyright 1978 by Associated Music Publishers, Inc.(BMI) International Copyright Secured. All rights reserved. Used by permission.

Example 5: Asko Concerto by Elliott Carter meas. 1-6

Asko Concerto, Copyright 2000 by Hendon Music, Inc. A Boosey & Hawkes Company. Copyrighted for all countries. All rights reserved. Reprinted by permission

Example 6: Boston Concerto by Elliott Carter meas. 1-4

Boston Concerto, Copyright 2002 by Hendon Music, Inc. A Boosey & Hawkes Company. Copyrighted for all countries. All rights reserved. Reprinted by permission.

Example 7: Boston Concerto by Elliott Carter meas. 14-19

Boston Concerto, Copyright 2002 by Hendon Music, Inc. A Boosey & Hawkes Company. Copyrighted for all countries. All rights reserved. Reprinted by permission.

BEGINNINGS AND ENDINGS—PLUS A CONVERSATION

Example 8: Dialogues for Piano and Orchestra by Elliott Carter meas. 12-18

Dialogues, Copyright 2003 by Hendon Music, Inc. A Boosey & Hawkes Company. Copyrighted for all countries. All rights reserved. Reprinted by permission.

ELLIOTT CARTER

Example 9: Dialogues for Piano and Orchestra by Elliott Carter meas. 19-24

CARTER: *Dialogues*

Dialogues, Copyright 2003 by Hendon Music, Inc. A Boosey & Hawkes Company. Copyrighted for all countries. All rights reserved. Reprinted by permission

Example 10: What Next? by Elliott Carter meas. 35-38

What Next?, Copyright 1999 by Hendon Music, Inc. A Boosey & Hawkes Company. Copyrighted for all countries. All rights reserved. Reprinted by permission.

ELLIOTT CARTER

Example 11: What Next? by Elliott Carter meas. 994-998

What Next?, Copyright 1999 by Hendon Music, Inc. A Boosey & Hawkes Company. Copyrighted for all countries. All rights reserved. Reprinted by permission.

for Yann Dubost
Gravitas
Seven Pieces for Double Bass

I.

Richard Wilson

Copyright © 2006 by Songs of Peer, Ltd.

ELLIOTT CARTER

* * * * *

Biography

Richard Wilson is the composer of some ninety works in many genres, including opera. He was the 2006/07 recipient of the Roger Sessions Memorial Bogliasco Fellowship. In 2004 he received an "Academy Award in Music" from the American Academy of Arts and Letters. He has previously received the Hinrichsen Award, the Stoeger Prize, the Cleveland Arts Prize, the Burge/Eastman Prize, a Frank Huntington Beebe Award, and a Guggenheim Fellowship. Recent commissions have come from the Koussevitzky and Fromm Foundations. His orchestral works have been performed by the San Francisco Symphony, the London Philharmonic, the American Symphony, the Pro-Arte Chamber Orchestra of Boston, the Orquesta Sinfonica de Colombia, the Residentie Orkest of The Hague, and the Hudson Valley Philharmonic A Phi Beta Kappa graduate of Harvard College, Mr. Wilson studied composition with Robert Moevs at Harvard, in Rome, and at Rutgers University. He studied piano in Cleveland, Aspen and New York City with Leonard Shure; and in Munich with Friedrich Wührer. Mr. Wilson holds the Mary Conover Mellon Chair in Music at Vassar, where he has taught since 1966; he is also Composer-in-Residence with the American Symphony Orchestra, for which he gives pre-concert talks.

Elliott Carter

(*A Centennial Tribute*)

John Ashbery

Having myself turned eighty this year, I am especially happy to note that Elliott Carter is inching toward his centenary, as wildly creative as ever. His ability to find new forms, new words (within his music, of course), is joyful news for all artists, I should think, but especially to older ones nearing the end of what are supposed to be their creative years. Now when people ask me if I'm still writing I can respond: "Yes, dammit, and so is Elliott!" In fact I heard from him the other day that he is again setting some of my poetry to music, as he did more than thirty years ago with *Syringa*.

The reason his music has always been an inspiration for me is that it says things that only poets are supposed to be able to say. I've always been drawn to the kind of expression that music attempts. Listening to great music gives us the impression that great ideas have been expressed, ones that are beyond the capacity of words. This is what inspires me to emulation—a hopeless task, since I am limited to working with words. Yet nothing else seems worth doing.

Years ago I attended the premiere of Elliott's *Duo for Violin and Piano* at Cooper Union. The violinist and pianist were placed at opposite ends of the wide stage, each seemingly playing his own score which occasionally intersected, or collided, with the other's. It seemed a metaphor for life—thinking one's thoughts, brooding, occasionally noticing the people around us and being forced to listen and be shaped in turn by what they are saying. A few months later I "coincidentally" wrote a long poem called *Litany*, two parallel columns of verse—sort of—meant to be considered simultaneously, another impossible task. (Of course it wasn't really a coincidence, but I didn't realize it at the time—that's often the way with influence—and only later saw how my experience of the *Duo* had given me that idea.)

That's only one of the gifts I have received, or taken, from this most verbal of musicians—make that "articulate." He somehow manages to conjure up precise shades of meaning that hitherto only great writers—Shakespeare or Henry James—have achieved, and all that without pronouncing a word (though of course he has done plenty of that in his essays, another story). Whenever I feel frustrated by the limitations of language, it's to his sublime discourse that I return and emerge from feeling refreshed yet again, awake to the possibilities of poetry.

Syringa

by John Ashbery

Orpheus liked the glad personal quality

Of the things beneath the sky. Of course, Eurydice was a part

Of this. Then one day, everything changed. He rends

Rocks into fissures with lament. Gullies, hummocks

Can't withstand it. The sky shudders from one horizon

To the other, almost ready to give up wholeness.

Then Apollo quietly told him: "Leave it all on earth.

Your lute, what point? Why pick at a dull pavan few care to

Follow, except a few birds of dusty feather,

Not vivid performances of the past." But why not?

All other things must change too.

The seasons are no longer what they once were,

But it is the nature of things to be seen only once,

ELLIOTT CARTER (*A CENTENNIAL TRIBUTE*)

As they happen along, bumping into other things, getting along

Somehow. That's where Orpheus made his mistake.

Of course Eurydice vanished into the shade;

She would have even if he hadn't turned around.

No use standing there like a gray stone toga as the whole wheel

Of recorded history flashes past, struck dumb, unable to

  utter an intelligent

Comment on the most thought-provoking element in its train.

Only love stays on the brain, and something these people,

These other ones, call life. Singing accurately

So that the notes mount straight up out of the well of

Dim noon and rival the tiny, sparkling yellow flowers

Growing around the brink of the quarry, encapsulizes

The different weights of the things.

                                       But it isn't enough

To just go on singing. Orpheus realized this

And didn't mind so much about his reward being in heaven

After the Bacchantes had torn him apart, driven

Half out of their minds by his music, what it was doing to them.

Some say it was for his treatment of Eurydice.

But probably the music had more to do with it, and

The way music passes, emblematic

Of life and how you cannot isolate a note of it

And say it is good or bad. You must

Wait till it's over. "The end crowns all,"

Meaning also that the "tableau"

Is wrong. For although memories, of a season, for example,

Melt into a single snapshot, one cannot guard, treasure

That stalled moment. It too is flowing, fleeting;

It is a picture of flowing, scenery, though living, mortal,

Over which an abstract action is laid out in blunt,

Harsh strokes. And to ask more than this

Is to become the tossing reeds of that slow,

Powerful stream, the trailing grasses

Playfully tugged at, but to participate in the action

No more than this. Then in the lowering gentian sky

Electric twitches are faintly apparent first, then burst forth

Into a shower of fixed, cream-colored flares. The horses

Have each seen a share of the truth, though each thinks,

"I'm a maverick. Nothing of this is happening to me,

Though I can understand the language of birds, and

The itinerary of the lights caught in the storm is fully apparent to me.

Their jousting ends in music much

As trees move more easily in the wind after a summer storm

And is happening in lacy shadows of shore-trees, now, day after day."

But how late to be regretting all this, even

Bearing in mind that regrets are always late, too late!

To which Orpheus, a bluish cloud with white contours,

Replies that these are of course not regrets at all,

Merely a careful, scholarly setting down of

Unquestioned facts, a record of pebbles along the way.

And no matter how all this disappeared,

Or got where it was going, it is no longer

Material for a poem. Its subject

Matters too much, and not enough, standing there helplessly

While the poem streaked by, its tail afire, a bad

Comet screaming hate and disaster, but so turned inward

That the meaning, good or other, can never

ELLIOTT CARTER

Become known. The singer thinks

Constructively, builds up his chant in progressive stages

Like a skyscraper, but at the last minute turns away.

The song is engulfed in an instant in blackness

Which must in turn flood the whole continent

With blackness, for it cannot see. The singer

Must then pass out of sight, not even relieved

Of the evil burthen of the words. Stellification

Is for the few, and comes about much later

When all record of these people and their lives

Has disappeared into libraries, onto microfilm.

A few are still interested in them. "But what about

So-and-so?" is still asked on occasion. But they lie

Frozen and out of touch until an arbitrary chorus

Speaks of a totally different incident with a similar name

In whose tale are hidden syllables

Of what happened so long before that

In some small town, one indifferent summer. †

---

†from *Houseboat Days*, published in *Selected Poems*, copyright (c) 1977, 1985 by John Ashbery. All rights reserved. Used by permission of Georges Borchardt, Inc. Literary Agency for the author.

ELLIOTT CARTER (*A CENTENNIAL TRIBUTE*)

* * * * *

Biography

John Ashbery was born in Rochester, New York in 1927. He earned degrees from Harvard and Columbia before travelling to France as Fulbright Scholar in 1955. Best known as a poet, he has published more than twenty collections, most recently *A Worldly Country* and *Notes from the Air: Selected Later Poems* (both Ecco/HarperCollins, 2007). He has served as Executive Editor of *ArtNews* and as art critic for *New York* magazine and *Newsweek*. His 1989-1990 Charles Eliot Norton lectures at Harvard were published as *Other Traditions* (Harvard, 2000). The winner of many prizes and awards, since 1990 he has been Charles P. Stevenson, Jr. Professor of Languages and Literature at Bard College. Additional information: www.flowchartfoundation.org/arc

In addition to Elliott Carter, many composers and musicians have worked with Ashbery's texts, including Laurie Anderson, Milton Babbitt, Antoine Beuger, James Dashow, John Duesenberry, Ricky Ian Gordon, Robin Holloway, Danielle Stech Homsy and Rio en Medio, Lee Hyla, Tania León, Daniel Levin, Peter Lieberson, Alvin Lucier, Stephen Malkmus and Pavement, Jeff Nichols, Paul Reif, Roger Reynolds, Lilia Rodionova, Ned Rorem, Eric Salzman, Mark Scearce, Mark So, Don Stewart, Joan Tower, Samuel Vriezen, Michael Webster, Scott Wheeler, Richard Wilson, Christian Wolff, Charles Wourinen, and John Zorn. Ashbery's deep interest in music and its relationship to his work is explored in his conversation with Sarah Rothenberg, available in the "Special Features" section of Bard College's Ashbery Resource Center website (address above).

Metric Modulation

Walter Zimmerman

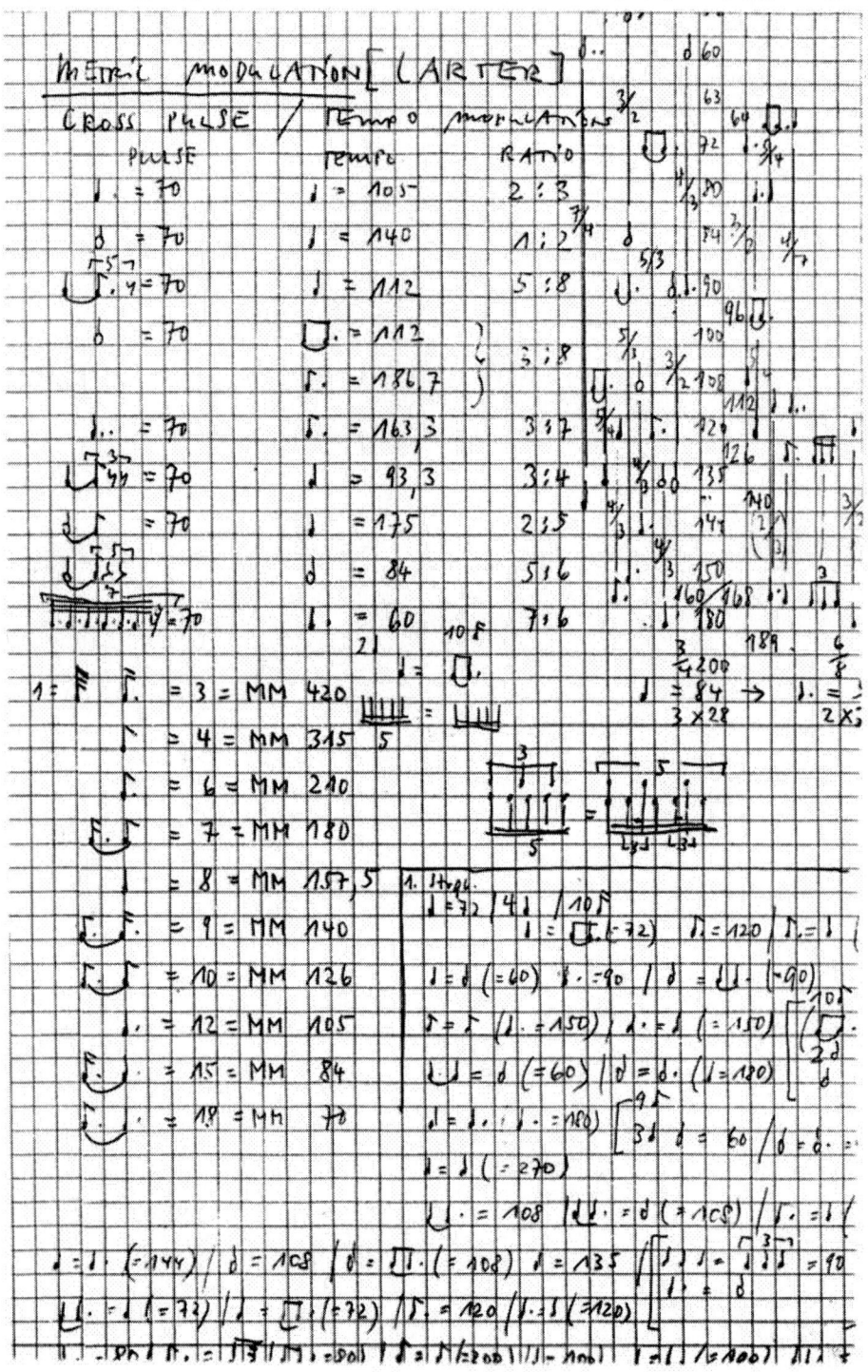

METRIC MODULATION

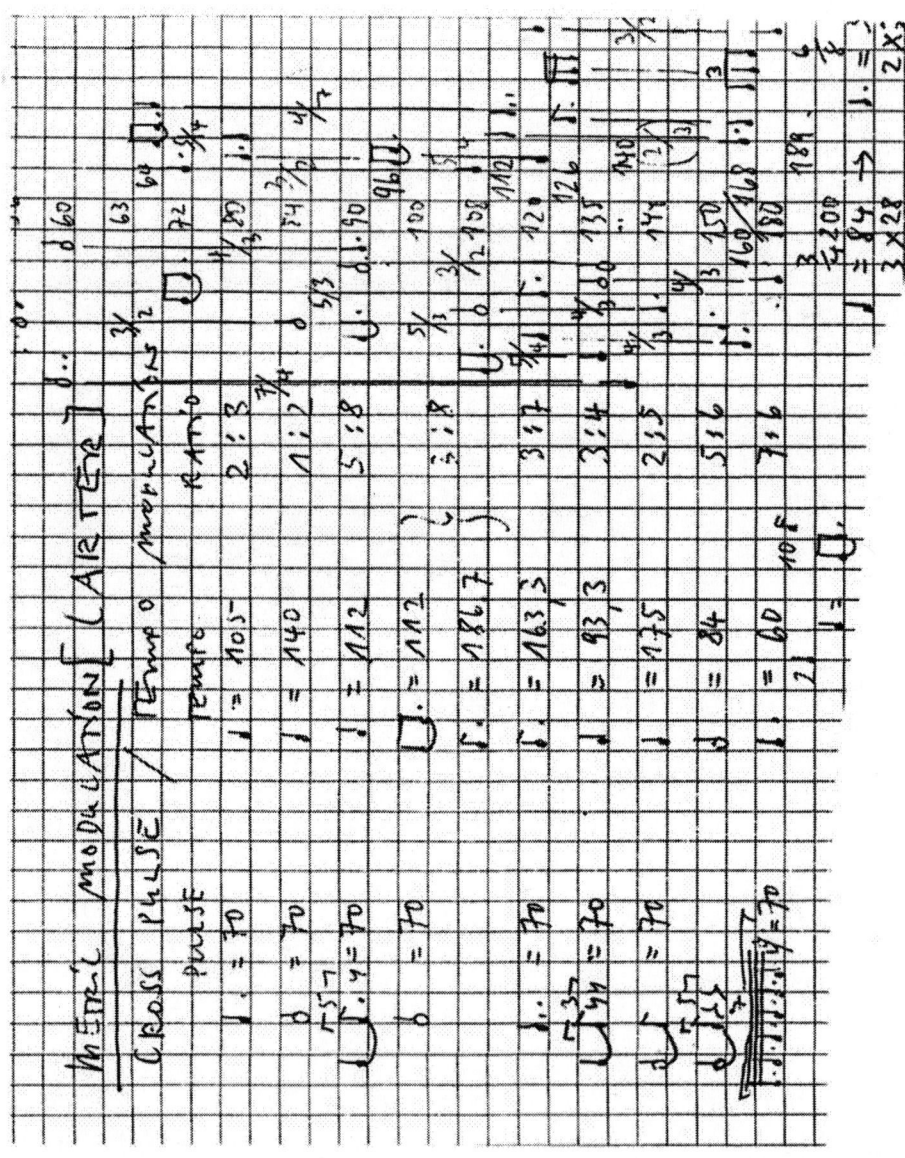

METRIC MODULATION

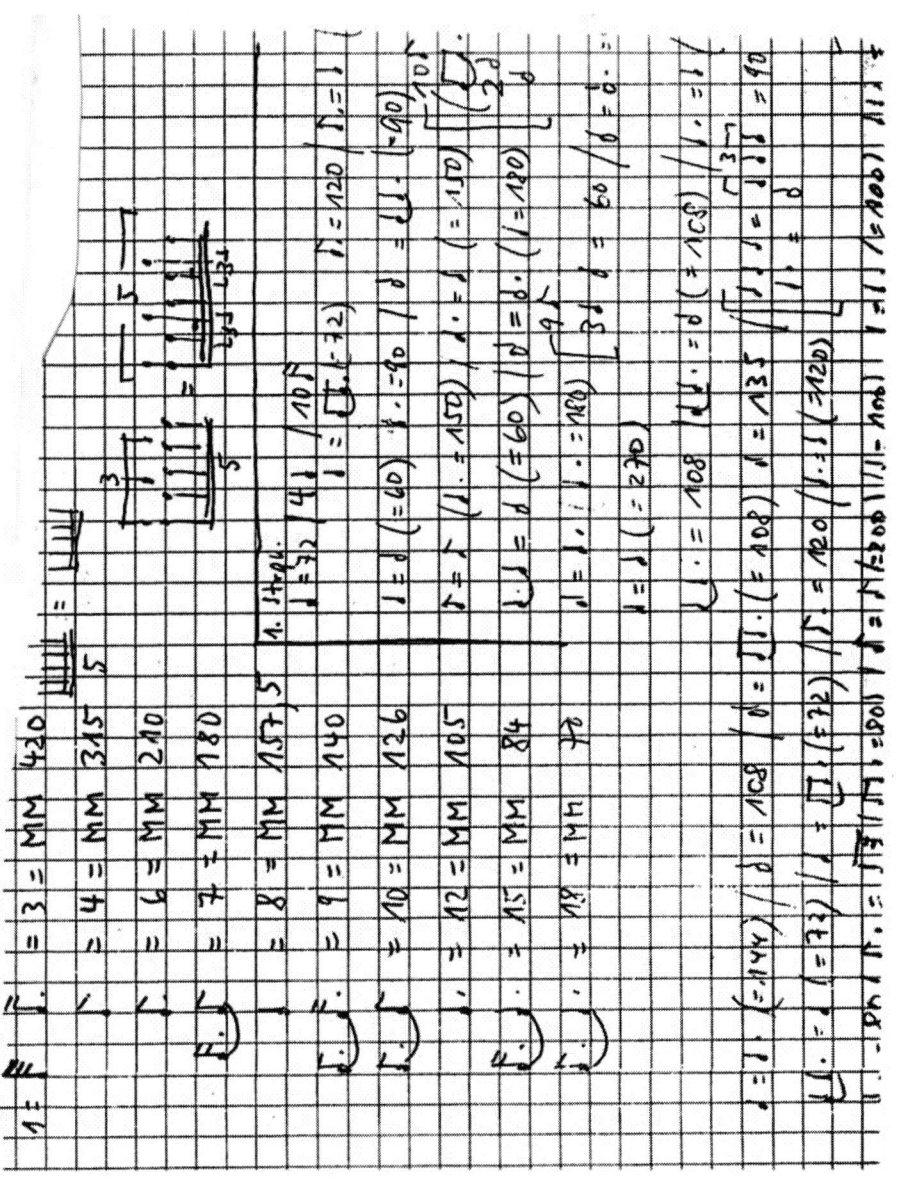

111

Elliott Carter String Quartet No. 1, I. Fantasia, measures 1 and 2

Copyright 1956 (Renewed) by Associated Music Publishers, Inc. (BMI) Internaytional Copyright Secured. All Rights Reserved. Used by Permission.

METRIC MODULATION

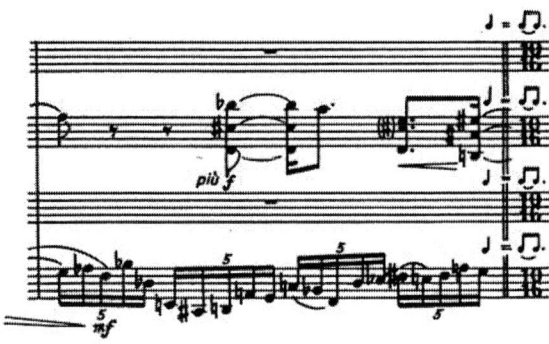

Measures 14 to 22

Measures 30 to 38

METRIC MODULATION

Measures 39 to 42

Measures 45 to 52

METRIC MODULATION

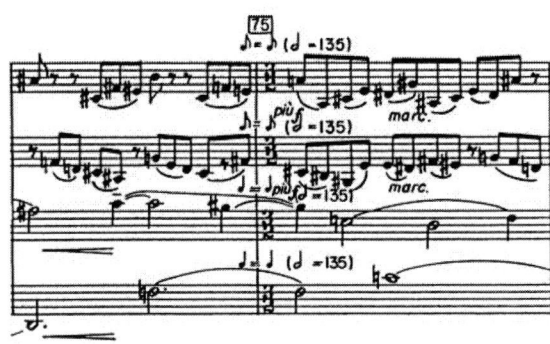

Meas. 74 to 81

"As I was Walking I came upon Chance" by Walter zimmerman, page 1

METRIC MODULATION

"As I was Walking I came upon Chance" by Walter zimmerman, page 2

* * * * *

Biography

Walter Zimmermann. German. Born Schwabach, Franconia, on April 15, 1949. Early studies of oboe, violin, piano; first compositions at age of 12. Composition studies with Werner Heider in Nuremberg , and pianist in Heider's ars nova ensemble, 1968-70. Briefly attended Mauricio Kagel's New Music Courses in Cologne. Studied simultaneously at the Institute for Sonology (Utrecht) and the Jaap-Kunst Ethnology Centre (Amsterdam) 1970-73. Computer studies in Hamilton USA, 1974; ethnological research, gathering folk music, especially from American Indian reservations, 1975-6. Founded Beginner Studio in Cologne 1977; organised concert series there till 1984. From 1982, composition teacher at the Liège Conservatoire, taught at Darmstadt Summer Courses 1982-84, teaching post at Royal Conservatoire den Haag 1988, from 1990 composition teacher in Karlsruhe, visiting professor at Folkwangshochschule 1992-93, from 1993 Professor of Composition at Berlin Academy of the Arts; he now lives in Berlin and Seidmar (Franconia). Awarded City of Cologne Förderpreis 1980, 'Ensemblia' first prize 1981, Villa Massimo stipendium (Rome) 1987, Schneider-Schott Prize 1989, Prix Italia 1990 for Die Blinden.

Chronological List of Works

1928	*My love is in a light attire* for voice and piano
1931	Incidental music for Sophocles' *Philoctetes* for baritone, tenor, men's chorus and chamber orchestra
1936	Incidental music for Plautus' *Mostellaria* for baritone, tenor, men's chorus and chamber orchestra
	Tarantella (finale to Mostellaria) for men's chorus and piano 4 hands or orchestra
1937	*Let's Be Gay* for women's chorus and 2 pianos
	Harvest home for chorus a cappella
	To Music for mixed chorus a cappella
1938	*Prelude, Fanfare and Polka* for small orchestra
	Tell Me Where Is Fancy Bred for alto voice and guitar
	Heart Not So Heavy As Mine for chorus cappella
1939	*Pocahontas* Ballet Legend in one act for orchestra
	Suite from Pocahontas Canonic Suite a. for quartet of alto saxophones b. revised for four clarinets (1956)
	Elegy a. for cello and piano b. for string quartet (1946) c. for string orchestra (rev. 1952) d. for viola and piano (rev. 1961)
1940	*Pastoral* for Viola/English Horn/Clarinet and Piano
1941	*The Defense of Corinth* for speaker, men's chorus and piano 4 hands
1942	*Symphony No. 1* for orchestra
	Three Poems by Robert Frost for voice and piano
1943	*Warble for Lilac time* for soprano/tenor and piano, or soprano and small orchestra
	Dust of Snow for violin and piano
	The Rose Family for voice and piano
	Voyage for medium voice and piano
1944	*The Difference* for soprano, baritone and piano
	Holiday Overture for orchestra
	The Harmony of Morning for women's chorus and chamber orchestra
1945	*Musicians Wrestle Everywhere* for chorus with optional string accompaniment
1946	*Piano Sonata*
1947	*The Minotaur* Ballet in one act and two scenes for orchestra
	Suite from The Meinotaur
	Emblems for men's chorus and piano solo

ELLIOTT CARTER

1948	*Woodwind Quintet*
	Sonata for violoncello and Piano
1949	*Eight Etudes and a Fantasy* for flute, oboe, clarinet and bassoon
1950	*Eight Pieces for Four Timpani*
	String Quartet No. 1
1952	*Sonata for Flute, Oboe, Cello and Harpsichord*
1953-1955	*Variations for Orchestra*
1959	*String Quartet No. 2*
1961	*Double Concerto for Harpsichord and Piano with two chamber orchestras*
1964	*Piano Concerto*
1966	*Adagio* and *Canto* for timpani
1969	*Concerto for Orchestra*
1971	*String Quartet No. 3*
	Canon for three equal Instruments "In Memoriam Igor Stravinsky"
1973	*Duo for Violin and Piano*
1974	*Brass Quintet*
	A Fantasy on Purcell's 'Fantasia on One Note' for brass quintet
1975	*A Mirror on Which to Dwell* for voice and large ensemble
	Three Poems of Robert Frost for voice and large ensemble
1976	*A Symphony of Three Orchestras*
1978	*Birthday FanfareSyringa*
1980	*Night Fantasies*
1981	*In Sleep, In Thunder*
1983	*Changes* for guitar
	Triple Duo for violin, cello, clarinet, flute, piano and percussion
1984	*Riconoscenza per Goffredo Petrassi* for solo violin
	Canon for 4 Homage to William Glock for flute, clarinet, violin and cello
1985	*Penthode* for five instrumental quintets
	Esprit rude/Esprit doux for flute and clarinet
1986	*A celebration of Some 100 X 150 Notes (Three Occasions)*
	String Quartet No. 4
1987	*Oboe Concerto*
1988	*Enchanted Preludes* for flute and cello
	Remembrance (Three Occasions)
	Birthday Flourish for five trumpets or brass quintet
1989	*Anniversary (Three Occasions)*
	Tempo e Tempi (1989-1999) for voice and ensemble

CHRONOLOGICAL LIST OF WORKS

1990	*Violin Concerto*
	Con Leggerezza Pensosa for clarinet, violin and cello
1991	*Scrivo in vento* flute solo
	Quintet for Piano and Winds (oboe, clarinet, bassoon, horn)
1992	*Trilogy* for oboe and harp
	Inner Song for oboe
	Immer Neu for oboe and harp
	Bariolage for harp
1993	*Partita (Symphonia: Sum Fluxae Pretiam Spei)*
	Gra for clarinet/trombone
1994	*90 +* piano solo
	Figment for cello
	Fragment No. 1 for string quartet
	Of Challenge and of Love Five Poems of John Hollander, soprano and piano
	Adagio tenebroso (Symphonia: Sum Fluxae Pretium Spei)
	esprit rude/esprit doux II for flute, clarinet and marimba
1995	*Figment* for cello solo *String Quartet No. 5*
1996	*Clarinet Concerto A 6*
	Letter Letter for english horn solo
	Allegro scorrevole (Symphonia: Sun Fluxae Pretium Spei)
1997	*Shard* for solo guitar
	Luimen for trumpet, trombone, harp, vibraphone, mandoline and guitar
	Quintet for Piano and String Quartet
	Symphonia Sum Fluxae Pretiam Spei
1998	*What's Next?* opera to a libretto by Paul Griffiths
1999	*Fragment No. 2* for string quartet
	Fantasy for violin
	Statement for violin
	Two Diversions for piano
2000	*Cello Concerto*
	ASKO Concerto for large ensemble (1999-2000)
	Retrouvailles for piano
2001	*Hiyoku* for two clarinets
	4 Lauds for violin (1984-2001)
	Figment II for cello
	Oboe Quartet for oboe, violin, viola and cello

	Rhapsodic Musings for violin
	Steep Steps for bass clarinet
2002	*Boston Concerto*
	Micomicon for orchestra
	Of Rewaking for mezzo soprano and orchestra
	Au Quai for bassoon and viola
	Retracing for bassoon
2003	*Dialogues* for piano and large ensemble
	Call for 2 trumpets and horn
2004	*Fons Juventatis* for orchestra
	More's Utopia for orchestra
	Three Illusions for Orchestra
	Mosaic for large ensemble
	Reflexions for large ensemble
2005	*Soundings* for orchestra
	Intermittences for piano
2006	*Horn Concerto*
	In the Distances of Sleep
	Catenaires for piano
2007	*Interventions* for piano and orchestra
	Mad Regales for chorus
	Clarinet Quintet for clarinet and string quartet
	Figment III for contrabass
	Figment IV for viola
	HBHH for oboe
	La Musique for mezzo-soprano solo
	Matribute for piano
	Sound Fields for string orchestra